Pub Strolls in
SHROPSHIRE

Robert Smart

COUNTRYSIDE BOOKS
NEWBURY BERKSHIRE

COUNTRYSIDE BOOKS
3 Catherine Road
Newbury, Berkshire

To view our complete range of books,
please visit us at
www.countrysidebooks.co.uk

ISBN 1 85306 789 X

Designed by Graham Whiteman
Photographs by the author

Typeset by Textype, Cambridge
Produced through MRM Associates Ltd., Reading
Printed by J. W. Arrowsmith Ltd., Bristol

Contents

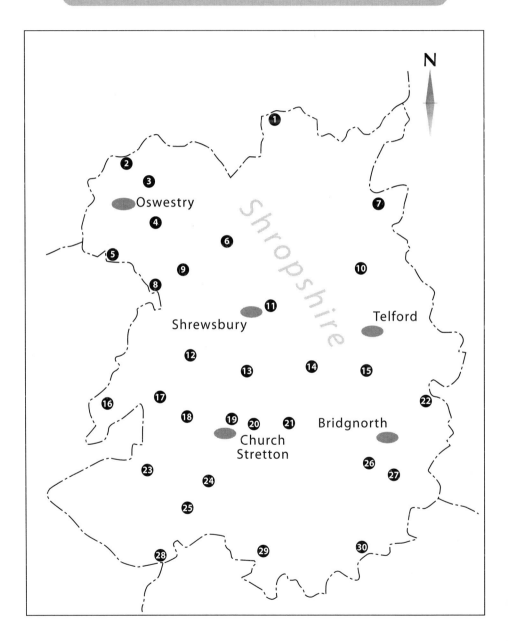

PUBLISHER'S NOTE

We hope that you obtain considerable enjoyment from this book; great care has been taken in its preparation. Although at the time of publication all routes followed public rights of way or permitted paths, diversion orders can be made and permissions withdrawn.

We cannot, of course, be held responsible for such diversion orders and any inaccuracies in the text which result from these or any other changes to the routes nor any damage which might result from walkers trespassing on private property. We are anxious though that all details covering the walks are kept up to date and would therefore welcome information from readers which would be relevant to future editions.

The simple sketch maps that accompany the walks in this book are based on notes made by the author whilst checking out the routes on the ground.

However, for the benefit of a proper map, we do recommend that you purchase the relevant Ordnance Survey sheet covering your walk. The Ordnance Survey maps are widely available, especially through booksellers and local newsagents.

One of England's most enchanting inland counties is Shropshire; a county of marked contrasts, from the splendid hill country of the south, with its streams and woods, to the wide open spaces of north Shropshire, with its fields, rivers and canals.

The hills of south Shropshire are its main attraction. The Stretton hills of Lawley, Caradoc and Long Mynd, together with the highly mysterious ridge of the Stiperstones and its association with witchcraft and the devil, make this the main walking area. However, north Shropshire, with its wide open plain, also has much to offer and so I have ensured there is a good balance of walks north of Shrewsbury as well – more than is usual in country books.

This diverse scenery also comes with a variety of pubs: from the plain homely to the more elaborate, from the remote country inn like the Horse Shoe at Bridges and the Royal Oak in Cardington; to the busy town pub such as the Unicorn at Ludlow and the canalside pub like the Jack Mytton at Hindford, where refreshments can be enjoyed while watching the colourful pageant of the passing barges. All the pubs welcome children and most have gardens and children's play areas. I looked especially for those pubs with a good ambience and a varied food menu.

These thirty, short circular walks will lead you to discover some of the hidden and lesser known parts of the county as well as the more popular tourist areas,

giving a variety of contrast and interest wherever you go. Walking in the country will inevitably involve crossing fields or using farm tracks which can, depending on the prevailing weather, be muddy, so always wear something sensible. On the whole, good strong walking shoes will be adequate as I have kept ground conditions very much in mind when planning the routes. Also, I find a good walking stick a useful but optional aid, particularly when negotiating a muddy patch or lane.

All the walks have been carefully selected with the word 'stroll' very much in mind. They vary from 1½ to 3½ miles and are eminently suitable for people of all ages whether walking alone or in company. Yet, they are long enough, and short enough, to justify a visit to the pub, as if an excuse was needed! All the walks start and finish at, or near, a public house with ample parking for cars. All the publicans I spoke to were most helpful and welcoming and, apart from Cleobury Mortimer, Ludlow, and Ironbridge, where there are public car parks nearby, they invite you to use their car park during your walk. However, it is only courteous to have a word with the landlord before setting off. And, after a leisurely stroll and a good lunch, perhaps a visit to one of the local attractions included in the book will serve to end a very pleasant day out.

Happy strolling!

Robert Smart

Whitchurch
The Willeymoor Lock Tavern

MAP: OS EXPLORER 257 (GR 535455) **WALK 1** DISTANCE: 2½ OR 3½ MILES

DIRECTIONS TO START: DRIVE NORTH ON THE A49 FROM SHREWSBURY. THE PUB IS 2 MILES NORTH OF WHITCHURCH; STAY ON THE A49, SIGNPOSTED 'WARRINGTON', **PARKING:** IN THE PUB CAR PARK (PATRONS), BUT YOU MUST ASK PERMISSION AS THE GATES MAY BE LOCKED WHEN THE PUB IS CLOSED. THE CAR PARK IS ACROSS THE CANAL, CONNECTED TO THE PUB BY A FOOTBRIDGE. APPROACH IS ALONG A SHORT TRACK OFF THE A49 AND SIGNED AT THE JUNCTION BY THE PUB'S NOTICE BOARDS.

This short and easy walk has something for all ages. It is level throughout and full of interest, with the constant passing of boats on this busy stretch of the canal. The return is over fields which are firm underfoot and easily walked. If you extend the route as far as the Grindley Locks (¹/₂ mile each way from point 2), you will find seats where you can relax and watch the boats ascend and descend the flight of locks. Whitchurch is situated in the Shropshire Plain, which here merges imperceptibly with the Cheshire Plain. Famous for its Shropshire Blue cheese and its clocks, which have been made in the town since 1690, Whitchurch displays a pleasing mix of old buildings from Tudor to Victorian and has been continually inhabited since Roman times.

The Willeymoor Lock Tavern

Of all the pubs in this book the Willeymoor must have the most romantic setting. Idyllically situated on the Shropshire Union Canal (Llangollen branch), it is well away from the busy A49, with its own approach road and a superb canalside location. It began life as a lock keeper's cottage and directly outside is the Willeymoor Lock. In summer you can sit on the terrace under the colourful sunshades and watch the boats as they rise and fall within the lock and enjoy, or join in, the friendly banter between the other spectators and the bargees. At one side is a delightful garden with picnic tables and a children's play area. Inside there are very comfortably furnished lounges with brocade wall seats, dimpled copper tables and two open fireplaces. A separate large dining room leads into the garden. At lunchtime a bar snacks menu offers sandwiches and jacket potatoes in addition to the main menu of steaks, grills, ham, chicken, fish dishes and salads. There are also vegetarian and children's menus. The beers are Timothy Taylor, Theakston and John Smith's, plus up to four guest ales, many from local Shropshire breweries; lagers and Strongbow cider are also available. The usual opening hours are kept, with food served from 12 noon to 2 pm daily, and from 6 pm to 9.30 pm on Tuesday to Saturday, 7 pm to 9 pm on Sunday and 6 pm to 9 pm on Monday. Telephone: 01948 663274.

The Walk

① From the pub turn right along the towpath for ¾ mile as far as bridge 26.

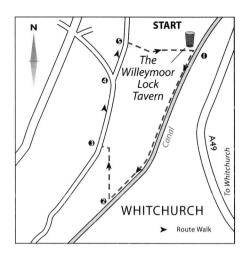

Here you can, if you wish, extend the walk by continuing along the towpath to Grindley Locks, ½ mile further on. Then return to this point.

② At the bridge turn to the right where you will find a waymarked stile. Cross the stile and fork half-right across the field to the next stile, also waymarked and clearly visible in the facing hedgerow. Cross the footbridge beyond and walk ahead with a fence and hedge on your left. Go through the next two gateways, where there may or may not be a gate. After the second gateway keep alongside the hedge on your left until you come to another waymarked stile. Cross this and turn right up a narrow field which gradually widens. Head towards the farmhouse and there is a stile near the far left-hand corner of the field. Cross the stile and turn left along a track.

③ Turn right along the lane, passing Holly Bank Farm.

④ At the road junction turn right downhill; there isn't any signpost but

The Shropshire Union canal

shortly you will pass a red brick cottage with a thick oak beam over the window.

⑤ You come to a junction by a yellow water hydrant sign. Turn right towards the farm, then pass to one side of the farm buildings and continue ahead on a dusty track which forks to the left by a red brick bungalow. Just before the gateway in front is a waymarked stile on the right-hand side. Cross the stile and fork diagonally left across the field to a second stile between two trees. Cross the stile and the pub is now directly in front of you. Head slightly left of a wooden electricity post in the middle of the field, beyond which is a stile

leading into a small 'paddock' alongside the pub garden. Cross the stile and then a second stile to return to the towpath and the pub.

PLACES OF INTEREST NEARBY

Beeston Castle – 8 miles north of Whitchurch via the A49 – an impregnable hilltop stronghold until it fell during the English Civil War. Superb views across the surrounding countryside for the price of a short climb, plus admission charge. In the care of English Heritage, there is an exhibition, also a gift shop and refreshments. Telephone: 01829 260464.

Chirk Bank
The Poachers Pocket

DIRECTIONS TO START: FROM OSWESTRY DRIVE NORTH ON THE A5 FOR 9 MILES. JUST AFTER THE LITTLE CHEF TAKE THE SECOND LEFT AT A ROUNDABOUT, SIGNED 'CHIRK BANK', AND THE PUB IS 200 YARDS ALONG ON THE LEFT. **PARKING:** IN THE PUB CAR PARK, WITH PERMISSION.

A stroll along the Shropshire Union Canal by way of an aqueduct some 70 feet above the fields below – combined with the views – makes this a stroll to be remembered. Built in 1800 by Thomas Telford, the aqueduct carries the canal high above the vale of the River Ceiriog while, at the same time, enabling you to cross from England into Wales. Alongside is the equally impressive viaduct, which takes the railway over the gap between the two countries. After crossing the aqueduct the walk drops down into the vale by way of a quiet back road, on the other side of which are the grounds of Chirk Castle. After crossing the river the walk returns on the edge of woods and across fields. It is an easy route and fairly level throughout.

The Poachers Pocket

Delightfully situated at the top of Chirk Bank, right by the canal towpath, the Poachers Pocket was originally a farmhouse and is around 200 years old. It is a fascinating place, all nooks and crannies. There are no less than five lounges (four non-smoking), on two levels, and all are very comfortable and compact, giving a sense of privacy in each. Outside is a two-level south-facing patio, with picnic tables where meals can be enjoyed in fine weather while canal boats pass by the other side of the wall. Alongside there is a well laid out play area. The food is excellent and the helpings copious. On offer are steaks, gammon, scampi, fish and chips, salads, Cajun chicken, lasagne and many other dishes. Vegetarians are well catered for and there is a separate children's menu. Banks's beers are served here, as well as Strongbow cider and two lagers. Food is available all day, every day from 11.30 am to 10 pm. Telephone: 01691 773250.

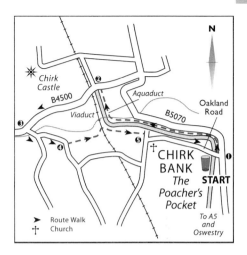

The Walk

① From the pub turn left up Oakland Road. Go to the right of the canal bridge and turn right along the towpath. Cross over the lane at bridge 21 and continue ahead. Soon you will cross the aqueduct and enter Wales. On reaching the other side you will see the 460 yards long Chirk Tunnel.

② You don't go through the tunnel but bear right up the tarmac path past the sign 'town centre 5 min walk'. On reaching the road at the top, turn left. Just here there is a viewpoint with a thoughtfully provided seat, giving you a great view of both the aqueduct and the viaduct. Now continue along the pavement, passing the signpost 'Dolywern B4500'. The road is fairly quiet and there is a good pavement.

③ Turn left at the signpost 'Weston Rhyn' and cross the bridge back into England! Walk up the hill as far as the first lane; here turn left by the weight restriction sign '3 tons except for access'.

④ Pass Yew Tree Cottage and after 50 yards bear left off the lane onto a level dirt track running between the trees with the river below you. This track soon emerges into a field at a stile. Turn left and walk alongside the fence on your left. Cross the railway by means of a flight of steps on each side – go carefully and listen for the warning klaxon from any approaching train. At the top of the steps on the other side cross a stile and follow a well-worn path along the left-hand edge of a large field. You will soon be able to see bungalows ahead. The field path ends just in front of a dormer-windowed bungalow.

The aquaduct and the viaduct

Cross the stile, a track and a second stile and walk along a short, narrow path between two bungalows to emerge into a lane.

⑤ Turn right up the lane and in no more than 50 yards, by a house called Highfields, turn left into Oakland Road again, and from here it's straight back to the pub.

PLACES OF INTEREST NEARBY

Chirk Castle (National Trust) – a maginificent fortress completed in 1310. Many state rooms are on view, richly furnished with tapestries and portraits. Formal gardens and open 18th century parkland put the castle in an idyllic setting. Telephone: 01691 777701.

Hindford
The Jack Mytton Inn

DIRECTIONS TO START: HINDFORD IS A MILE NORTH OF THE A495 BETWEEN ELLESMERE AND WHITTINGTON. TURN OFF WHEN SIGNPOSTED 'JACK MYTTON INN', 3 MILES SOUTH-WEST OF ELLESMERE. **PARKING:** PATRONS ARE WELCOME TO USE THE INN CAR PARK WHILE WALKING; PLEASE MENTION THIS TO THE LANDLORD.

This lovely North Shropshire walk is level throughout, the route taking you along the towpath of the Shropshire Union Canal, Llangollen branch, across a field and then back along a quiet country lane. The hamlet of Hindford consists of the pub and a few houses and cottages grouped around the junction of lanes in the middle. On a clear day there are good views south across the flat countryside to the Breidden Hills beyond Melverley and the Welsh Mountains to the west. A more restful, tranquil place than Hindford would be difficult to find.

The Jack Mytton Inn

This canalside pub is in a most attractive setting, with a spacious lawn and picnic tables alongside the towpath but separated from it by a hedge so that it is quite safe for children. Originally a farmhouse, it probably came into the licensed trade as a result of its proximity to the canal and the latter's need for a refreshments stop for bargees. The name commemorates the flamboyant Shropshire squire Jack Mytton, a 19th century landowner renowned for his drunken exploits. A feature of this inn is its outside bar which serves directly onto the lawns. Inside there is a compact bar, and behind that the lounge with extremely comfortable settees and an open fireplace in the corner. The restaurant, which is a no-smoking area, has a double door that opens onto the back lawn. A comprehensive menu lists a variety of starters, fish and meat dishes, among them scampi, cod, curry, lasagne, duck, gammon and chicken chasseur. The bar food includes jacket potatoes and baguettes, and there is also a specials board. A roast is offered on Sundays. Timothy Taylor and Salopian Mad Jack are among the beers served, plus two guest beers which change frequently. The opening times are 12 noon to 3 pm and 6 pm to 11 pm, or all day if the demand is there, with food available from 12 noon to 2.30 pm and 7 pm to 9.30 pm. Telephone: 01691 679861.

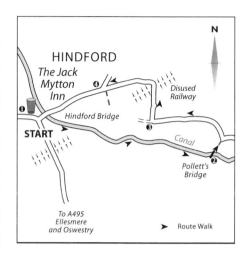

The Walk

① Cross the pub car park and exit through the archway onto the canal towpath. There are usually several longboats moored here, making a very attractive sight with their many different colours. Turn right along the towpath and pass under the roadbridge. A quarter of a mile on you pass between the abutments of the former Cambrian Railway line which crossed the canal at this point. In its heyday this was the main Cambrian line and carried trains from Manchester to Aberystwyth, through Oswestry and Welshpool, but then a new line was built between Welshpool and Shrewsbury and this part of the system became little more than a branch line. It closed in 1965. Continue along the towpath, passing under bridge 8, Paddock Bridge, and then bridge 7, Broom's Bridge; the numbers are over the arch on the other side of the bridge.

② At bridge 6, Pollet's Bridge, the towpath is blocked by iron fencing and you have to leave the towpath anyway. Turn right and cross the canal by the overbridge, going to a waymarked stile on the other side. Cross the stile and turn right around

The attractive gardens of the Jack Mytton Inn

the edge of a field with the hedge on your right. It is only a short way to the stile which you will find ahead of you; cross this and turn left in the lane.

③ At a sharp right-hand corner near a wooden electricity pylon follow the lane round to the right; don't go straight ahead on the dirt track which only leads to a farmhouse. The lane now rises gently to cross the Cambrian Railway again, this time by an overbridge above a deep cutting. It is from this lane that you get the best views south to the Breidden Hills above Melverley. Continue along this quiet back lane and enjoy the peace and quiet of this part of Shropshire.

④ At the junction of roads continue ahead, signposted 'Oswestry'. This will take you back to the pub.

PLACES OF INTEREST NEARBY

Park Hall Farm, Oswestry (GR 305316), just off the A5 bypass north of the town – a day out for all the family, with a collection of vintage cars and motorbikes, animal paddocks, quad bike driving, cart rides and other attractions, also a gift shop. Telephone: 01691 671123.

Queen's Head
The Queen's Head

MAP: OS EXPLORER 240 (GR 338268)	**WALK 4**	DISTANCE: 2 MILES

DIRECTIONS TO START: QUEEN'S HEAD IS JUST 2 MILES SOUTH-EAST OF OSWESTRY VIA THE A5 ROAD TO SHREWSBURY. THE PUB IS A LARGE WHITE BUILDING CLEARLY VISIBLE FROM THE MAIN ROAD WHICH NOW BYPASSES THE VILLAGE. **PARKING:** PATRONS ARE WELCOME TO USE THE PUB CAR PARK WHILE WALKING, BUT PLEASE ASK FIRST. THERE IS A PUBLIC CAR PARK OPPOSITE.

In the 1990s the route of the A5 was changed and the hamlet of Queen's Head, which consists of the pub and a few houses, is now a good deal quieter than it once was. The Queen's Head itself was originally a coaching inn on Thomas Telford's road from London to Holyhead, which in its turn was built on the foundations of Watling Street, the Roman road. Later still, around 1790, came the Shropshire Union Canal, here the Montgomery branch, and this added to the fortunes of the pub, which with its roadside and canalside location was a stopover for both modes of transport. This pleasant, level stroll crosses several fields before returning to the pub along the towpath of the recently restored canal.

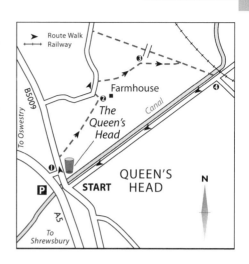

The Queen's Head

This superb pub has two very comfortably furnished non-smoking lounges, one of which has a conservatory overlooking the canal. Both bars are decorated in restful pastel shades, making the whole place very welcoming. Outside there are tables on the small lawn and terrace. The menu is vast, no less than three blackboards setting out the gastronomic delights awaiting you – from the exotic, such as duck with blackberry and vodka sauce, to plain English cooking. A variety of sandwiches and jacket potatoes, vegetarian food, pizzas and desserts are also on offer. The ales are Theakston Best Bitter and Old Peculier, locally brewed Proud Salopian and also a guest beer, such as Hopping Mad from the Wood's Wistanstow brewery (see Walk 24). The pub is open all day from 11 am and food is available from noon until 9.30 pm. Telephone: 01691 610255, website www.queensheadshrops.co.uk

The Walk

① Turn right from the pub and walk north, signposted 'Whittington 3'. This is the former A5, before it was diverted. Where the hedge on the right ends, cross a waymarked stile into a small field and head for the gate on the other side. Now cross another stile into a very large field and turn right. Make your way towards the wooden electricity pylon in the middle of the field, and passing about 20 yards to the right of it you should come directly to the next stile, with Wootton Farm across to your right.

② In the lane turn left and then at the next road junction, by Oak Tree Cottage,

turn right. Walk along this lane for about 50 yards until you find a stile on the right. Cross the stile and walk ahead, bearing slightly left. You will soon see a dirt track coming from the farm and crossing your path. When you get to it you will see a waymark post and another post with a water tap on it. Turn left along the track.

③ Go through a double width field gate and walk on alongside the fence on your right. Across to your left is the railway and you should be able to see a grey box on the embankment ahead to your left; the way out of the field is near that box but for the moment stay near the fence. When you reach a copse on the other side of the fence

PLACES OF INTEREST NEARBY

Hen Dinas or **Old Oswestry**, as it is now known, just north of Oswestry town (GR 295310). A formidable fort created during the Iron Age, it is now an open space of five concentric rings with superb views. Legend has it that King Arthur's bride Guinevere was born here. In the care of English Heritage and always open.

A restful view of the canal

bear half-left towards a clump of trees, beyond which is a white cottage with a grey roof. Just to the left of the trees is a waymarked field gate. Go through and, passing the cottage, come to the canal.

④ Cross the bridge and turn left to gain the towpath, then go left under the bridge. On arriving back at Queen's Head you will find a flight of steps on the left to take you up to the lane which has been parallel to the towpath since point 4. Cross the bridge to return to the car park.

Pant
The Cross Guns

MAP: OS EXPLORER 240 (GR 273220)   WALK 5   **DISTANCE:** 2½ MILES

DIRECTIONS TO START: PANT IS 5 MILES SOUTH OF OSWESTRY ON THE A483 ROAD TO WELSHPOOL. THE PUB IS ON THE RIGHT-HAND SIDE AS YOU ENTER THE VILLAGE.
PARKING: IN THE PUB CAR PARK, WITH PERMISSION.

This is a superb walk in any weather conditions. It first uses a canal towpath to reach the next village of Llanymynech, and then a quiet back lane to join a stretch of the Offa's Dyke long-distance footpath. You then return along on easy, level footpaths through a disused quarry which nature has reclaimed for its own. Because of the underlying limestone the ground is rarely soggy or unduly muddy but mostly, especially through the quarry and along the towpath, dry underfoot. This is a delightful walk for bird lovers as the woods around the quarry are ideal for the many species that love thick undergrowth. The walk actually crosses the border into Wales, as you will see on the return leg when you come to the 'Welcome to Shropshire' sign, indicating that you have been over the border without knowing it. Like so much of the county, this area has had much industrial activity in its past and traces of this will be seen on the walk. You will also pass a noticeboard with a history of the Llanymynech Heritage Area (entry by permit) by the canal.

The Cross Guns

Situated on the main road in the linear village of Pant, the Cross Guns presents an attractive sight. On one side is a large garden with picnic tables and a children's play area while behind it is the village bowling green. In front of the pub is a large conservatory which adds extra dining space to the very comfortably furnished lounge. A good-sized menu offers large and small meals according to taste – an ample range of meat and fish dishes, salads and grills, supplemented by a children's menu. There is also a Sunday roast. The real ales are Banks's Bitter and Marston's Pedigree and Bitter, while Stella Artois is also on tap, together with Scrumpy Jack cider. Opening hours are 12 noon to 3 pm and 7 pm to 11 pm on Monday to Thursday and all day on Friday and Saturday. Food is available from 12 noon to 3 pm and 7 pm (5.30 pm on Saturday) to 9.30 pm on Monday to Saturday and all day on Sunday. Telephone: 01691 830821.

The Walk

① From the pub turn right. At the sign 'Methodist Chapel' cross the road and descend Rhiew Revel Lane. Cross the canal bridge and turn left for the towpath and left again under the bridge, opposite the remains of limestone ovens. The canal here is not in working order but I am told that restoration is planned.

② Continue along the towpath until you reach the roadbridge on the outskirts of Llanymynech. Go up to the road and turn right.

③ Cross the road when safe to do so and at the '40' sign fork left into a quiet narrow lane, signposted to Pen-y-Foel. At a right-hand bend you pass the first of the Offa's Dyke signposts – the path is marked with a white acorn on a black background. Follow the lane round towards Pen-y-Foel Cottages. Just beyond, fork right at a second Offa's Dyke signpost. The lane rises steeply to the edge of the woods.

④ Cross a stile by the last cottage and follow a track through the woods past the sign 'Private Land please keep to the footpaths'. Cross a second stile, marked with a yellow arrow, and continue ahead. At a crossing of paths with a signpost, go straight ahead, leaving the Offa's Dyke Path which continues to your left. Go on until you come to a junction of paths by an old quarry building covered with ivy; here join a wide track with a waymark post 'Arls Summit'.

⑤ Turn right and follow the wide path which wends its way beneath the sheer rock face of the quarry on your left. Stay on this

Along the canal towpath

path now, ignoring all sidetracks. At a facing gate turn left to another gate just below, a bridleway gate. Here turn right and walk along a level track through a wooden kissing gate. Turn left over the first stile and cross the field diagonally to a metal kissing gate. This leads into the children's playground you passed on the way out. At the main road turn left for the pub.

PLACES OF INTEREST NEARBY

The Llanymynech Heritage Area is passed on the right (across the canal, via a footbridge), just after the former railway bridge. It consists of a complex of limekilns and marked walks, but an entry permit is required. This can be obtained from The Countryside Service, Swan Hill, Ellesmere, SY12 0DQ. Telephone: 01691 623461.

Myddle
The Red Lion

MAP: OS EXPLORER 241 (GR 468239)   WALK 6   DISTANCE: 2 MILES

DIRECTIONS TO START: FROM SHREWSBURY TAKE THE A528 ELLESMERE ROAD. MYDDLE IS 7 MILES NORTH-WEST OF SHREWSBURY; TURN LEFT WHEN YOU SEE THE SIGNPOST. THE PUB IS IN THE MIDDLE OF THE VILLAGE. **PARKING:** IN THE PUB CAR PARK, WITH PERMISSION. PLEASE USE THE SIDE OR REAR CAR PARK.

This is a very pleasant, easy and level walk across fields and along a green lane. Gentle rolling farmland surrounds you on every side, while in the distance the hills of South Shropshire and the Breiddens add an attractive backdrop to this delightful rural scene. Although Myddle is situated in the North Shropshire plain which is relatively flat, hills are never far away, the nearest being Harmer Hill, the source of much of the red sandstone used to build the pub, the church and many houses and garden walls in this charming village.

The Red Lion

Of all the pubs I've visited I doubt if any has a more interesting history than the attractive Red Lion; you can read all about it in a framed drawing on the wall of the main bar – it must be one of the earliest 'barn conversions' ever. The original part of the pub, the half-timbered area, was originally the rector's tithe barn which stood by the church lychgate. Early in the 17th century, it was moved to its present location. The interior is very comfortable and spacious, with beamed ceilings and a large open fireplace separating the bar from the non-smoking restaurant. Menus vary according to the season and available ingredients, as all meals are freshly prepared. Lunchtime bar snacks with generous portions include scampi, plaice, lasagne, ploughman's and sandwiches, and there is an extensive evening menu. Beers on offer include Marston's Pedigree, Banks's Bitter and Kronenbourg and Foster's lagers, alongside Woodpecker and Strongbow cider. Normal opening times apply and meals are served at lunchtime from 12 noon to 2 pm and in the evenings (not Mondays) from 7 pm to 8.30 pm. Telephone: 01939 290951.

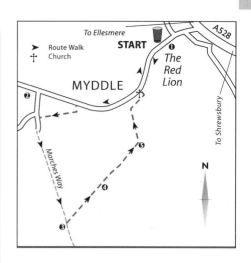

The Walk

① From the pub turn right along the road. Pass the church and walk out of the village. About 50 yards after the last house on the left, at the rear of the '30' speed limit sign, go through a gate into the field and turn right (ignore the signpost arm pointing to the left; that is a different path). Walk round the edge of the field, keeping the hedge on your right, to emerge onto a green lane by a stile.

② Turn left and walk along the green lane for ¹/₂ mile; it may be a bit muddy in places after rain but there is usually a good verge to help get past any such patches. Ignore the waymarked stile which you will see on the first right-hand bend and stay on the green lane until you come to the second waymark.

③ Turn left at the signpost and cross a sturdy footbridge and stile. Cross the field in the direction shown by the signpost arm. Continue towards an obvious gap in the distant hedgerow where there is a waymarked field gate. While walking across this and the next field you get the best views south to the distant hills.

④ Go through the gate and continue ahead, now with the church tower ahead of you and a hedge on your left. After passing through the next gate you join a concrete track which leads to the farm, but you do not go as far as that.

The church at Myddle

⑤ Look for the stile about 100 yards along the concrete track – it is marked with two waymark signs. Take the footpath going right, across the fields towards the church; there is a stone stile in the wall surrounding the churchyard, just to the right of the church tower. Cross the stile and at the churchyard path turn right. In the lane leading to the farm turn left, and then go right when you reach the road for the walk back through the village to the pub.

PLACES OF INTEREST NEARBY

Hawkstone Park, Hodnet (GR 580291) – 3 miles east of Myddle – a privately owned country park, with many walks, hidden pathways, concealed grottos, secret tunnels, follies and a 'Nelson's Column' type monument, with views from the top of thirteen counties. Special event weekends are held each month throughout the summer. Tea room, gift and book shop. Telephone: 01939 200311.

Goldstone Wharf, Cheswardine
The Wharf Tavern

DIRECTIONS TO START: FROM MARKET DRAYTON DRIVE SOUTH FOR 2 MILES ON THE A529 TOWARDS NEWPORT. TAKE THE THIRD TURNING ON THE LEFT, SIGNED FIRST 'GOLDSTONE', THEN 'GOLDSTONE WHARF'. **PARKING:** IN THE PUB CAR PARK, WITH PERMISSION.

Although North Shropshire is mainly flat, this area around Cheswardine is an exception and from the walk there are superb views south across the low lands to the South Shropshire hills. If you want peace and quiet this stroll from Goldstone Wharf is specially made for you and it is full of contrasts, partly along a canal towpath, partly on quiet country lanes and partly across fields. Cheswardine village is an interesting place, in particular note the unusual wrought iron street furniture, including the tall flower stands topped with animals, butterflies and swans. One of many wrought iron seats is outside the post office, with water churns painted in canal boat fashion, the brewer's dray opposite and the years of Best Kept Village competition wins proudly displayed – watching over it all, the church of St Swithin stands on a prehistoric site with an adjacent moated motte.

The Wharf Tavern

There is something about canalside pubs – they seem to go out of their way to be extremely attractive, outside and in – and this is no exception. The large, beautifully groomed lawns which stretch down to the water's edge and sport a host of picnic tables for outside meals on sunny days enhance its ideal location. Sliding doors open directly from the restaurant onto this panorama so that you can have a great view from the inside too. Built at the time of the canal, the Wharf has always been an inn, and the warmth of welcome is only surpassed by the food on offer. You can choose from dishes such as homemade steak and kidney pie, omelettes, grills of salmon, gammon and steaks, and there are always various salads, as well as vegetarian and children's menus. Beers include Caffrey's, Worthington and a guest ale, and Guinness, Grolsch and Carling lager and Scrumpy Jack cider are also available. The usual opening hours are kept and food is served from 12 noon to 2 pm and 7 pm to 9.30 pm every day. Advance booking is a good idea at holiday weekends as it is an extremely popular place. A caravan site is attached to the pub. Telephone: 01630 661226.

The Walk

① From the car park turn right to cross the canal bridge and then turn left through a pedestrian gate to descend to the towpath at bridge 55. Turn right and walk away from the pub along the towpath, under bridge 54 to bridge 53 (neither of these is numbered).

② At bridge 53, where there is a notice 'Hodnet Anglers Club', go under the bridge and then turn right up the steps to a gate which leads into the lane. Turn right and walk up the lane, passing a white house on the left, Westcott.

③ On the edge of the village, turn left – The Westfields. Go straight on past Donaldson Drive, through barriers across the path and turn right at the next track, passing the children's playground on your right and then the village hall.

④ Turn left into High Street. The old brewer's dray is on the corner of Symons Way, and notice that even the litter bins are in wrought iron. Go straight on up the hill and past the church. Turn left along Haywood Lane. The views of the distant hills to your left include the Wrekin with its TV mast on the peak, while further south is Caer Caradoc and to the right the Long Mynd.

⑤ Well clear of the village, and after passing two isolated cottages on your right,

Colourful boats line the banks of the canal

just before a block of council houses on the left, turn left at a stile. Go down the field with the back gardens of the houses on your right and then pass a water pumping station and a pond. Go through a field gate and continue with the hedge on your right. Cross two stiles and turn left around the edge of a tree plantation. When you come to the gateway, turn left and head for the canal, visible between the rows of trees. When you see the bridge to your right, turn right.

⑥ Cross the bridge and turn right through a small copse by way of a curving path which takes you back to the towpath. Turn left now to return to the pub.

PLACES OF INTEREST NEARBY

Market Drayton – an interesting and attractive market town with many half-timbered buildings and famed for its gingerbread. Also popular are the pies based on a secret recipe associated with Robert Clive, the famous Clive of India, who lived here as a boy; both the church and grammar school have connections with him. Telephone: 01630 652139 (tourist information centre).

Melverley
The Tontine Inn

MAP: OS EXPLORER 240 (GR 334167)   WALK 8   DISTANCE: 2½ OR 3¾ MILES

DIRECTIONS TO START: FROM SHREWSBURY TAKE THE A458 WELSHPOOL ROAD. JUST AFTER THE VILLAGE OF FORD, TURN RIGHT ON THE B4393, SIGNPOSTED 'FOUR CROSSES'. AT CREWE GREEN TURN RIGHT, SIGNPOSTED 'MELVERLEY 1'.
PARKING: PATRONS ARE WELCOME TO USE THE PUB CAR PARK WHILE WALKING; PLEASE ASK THE LANDLORD.

This is a favourite walk of mine. There are lots of stiles but the route is level throughout, and right from the outset you will be enchanted by the view as you walk along the flood bank of the River Vrynwy – the river forms the boundary between England and Wales – and look across to the west, an uninterrupted vista of fields and hills. In addition to the scenery, I particularly like the flood banks, called 'argae', built in 1790, which give dry conditions underfoot – except after flooding of course! The Breidden Hills, crowned with the monuments erected to commemorate Admiral Lord Rodney's victories over the French, are just across the vale, while in the distance the mountains of Wales complete the picture. Melverley is famed for its church, a most beautiful building entirely of timber with a wattle and daub infill, dating from 1406 and a perfect example of Tudor construction. A short cut is available if you wish (see map).

The Tontine Inn

Although Melverley is such a small place, it has one of the finest pubs for miles around, renowned for the quality of its food. The lounge bars are extremely comfortable – a small TV lounge with easy chairs and a fascinating main lounge area with various antiques hanging from the beams: historic cameras, oil lamps, harness, antique aeroplanes, numerous photographs of old Shrewsbury, the list is endless. There is a no-smoking dining area in the conservatory with a south-facing aspect, looking out onto the garden. Meals can also be taken outside in fine weather, while children can enjoy themselves on the swings. Specialities are the Tuesday 'Steak Night' and the Sunday lunches for which advance booking is essential. The menu is vast, with both plain English and exotic cooking well represented, plus lunchtime sandwiches, baguettes, ploughman's and much more. In addition there are vegetarian and children's menus (the full food list is shown on the website). The beers on offer include Worthington, Morland Old Speckled Hen and a summertime guest beer; Carling lager and Scrumpy Jack and Dry Blackthorn cider are also served. Overnight accommodation is available too. The opening hours on Monday to Saturday are 12 noon to 3 pm and 7 pm (6 pm on Tuesday, Friday and Saturday) to 11 pm. On Sunday the pub is open from 12 noon to 3.30 pm only. Telephone: 01691 682258, website www.tontineinn.co.uk

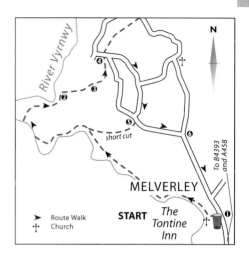

The Walk

① Turn left from the front door of the pub along the lane to the church. Go into the churchyard and turn right to a little gate. Go through and walk along the flood bank for 2 miles, passing over nine stiles. There is a short cut along a track after the sixth stile, but I advise taking it only if the weather is dry (rain makes it very muddy further on); it takes you to point 5.

② You come to a ruin just beyond a tenth stile. Here leave the 'argae' and drop down to a waymarked stile. Go straight across the field in the direction shown by the arrow, heading just to the left of a solitary tree to where there is a kink in the field boundary. Cross the drainage ditch by a plank bridge to a second waymarked stile. It is sobering to think that during flood conditions the top of this stile is underwater! I have seen flotsam in the hedge above the height of the stile – and at this distance from the river too!

③ Go straight over the next field to the gate ahead, no stile. Go through and then

The River Vrynwy and the Breidden Hills

turn right in just a few yards over a waymarked stile. In the third field turn hard left to a second waymarked stile. You will see some farm buildings through the trees to your right. Cross the plank bridge and the next stile and continue ahead in a small field to the next stile. Cross this into a narrow field and so to the last stile just in front of you.

④ Turn right along the lane. Don't take the first turning on the left; continue ahead and pass Hendre Farm.

⑤ You come to a crossroads of three lanes and the grassy track from the river. There is no signpost but you will see a no through road sign to the right and a stile opposite you. Turn left and walk along the lane until you come to the T junction with a signpost pointing back the way you've come which says 'Hendre'.

⑥ Turn right and continue for ¼ mile to return to the pub.

PLACES OF INTEREST NEARBY

The Welshpool & Llanfair Railway (GR 216076) – a 2 foot 6 inch narrow gauge steam railway, one of the famous 'little railways of Wales' – runs from the western outskirts of Welshpool along the vale of the River Banwy, using locomotives and rolling stock from many European and African railways. Telephone: 01938 810441, website www.wllr.org.uk

Nesscliffe
The Old Three Pigeons

DIRECTIONS TO START: NESSCLIFFE IS 8 MILES NORTH-WEST OF SHREWSBURY, JUST OFF THE A5. THE PUB IS ON THE LEFT-HAND SIDE IN THE CENTRE OF THE VILLAGE.
PARKING: PATRONS ARE WELCOME TO USE THE LARGE CAR PARK BEHIND THE PUB WHILE WALKING, BUT PLEASE MENTION THIS INSIDE.

Although situated in the North Shropshire plain, this walk is upon one of the many sandstone outcrops peculiar to this part of the county, a complete contrast to most other walks north of Shrewsbury. From the village, the canopy of pine trees conceals the delights of Nesscliffe Hill. Here we have a pleasant, easy stroll, sweet with the scent of pine, along sandy tracks, through thickets of rhododendrons and outcrops of sandstone rocks. An Iron Age hill fort, old quarry workings and the cave of the infamous local 15th century outlaw Humphrey Kynaston are three of the interesting attractions of the walk, and there are stupendous views from the several vantage points. The route does involve a climb at the start but once up the effort is well rewarded.

The Old Three Pigeons

Superb is the word that comes to mind. On the right as you enter there is the very large bar area with its large inglenook fireplace where Humphrey Kynaston is reputed to have sat. The immediate bar area itself is part of the original building as is the dining area in front of you, and finally on the left is a large restaurant (non-smoking). Outside, the garden has tables for a hot day. The inn was originally built in 1403 to serve the Irish mail coaches, for this was the main road from London to Holyhead. A very friendly resident ghost is often to be seen, though he never strays beyond where was once the back door. The food is excellent – not only is there a vast choice, but so much is home-made, sausages, bacon, gammon and bread, to name but a few, are all made on the premises, while the fish arrives daily from the Birmingham fish market. Children and vegetarians are well catered for too. The beers include John Smith's Extra Smooth and guests, alongside Carling lager, Murphy's and Dry Blackthorn cider. The Old Three Pigeons is open daily, usual hours (all day at weekends). Food is available from 12 noon to 2.30 pm and 6 pm to 9.30 pm, and at other times by prior arrangement; just telephone and every effort will be made to accommodate you (large parties should always book in advance). Telephone: 01743 741279.

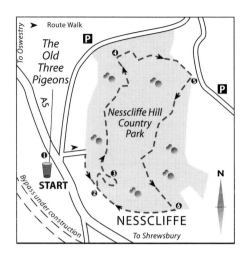

The Walk

① From the pub cross the road to the lane signposted 'Hopton'. Go through the gate on the right, 'Nesscliffe Hill Country Park'.

An information board inside is worth reading. Follow the track uphill and the signs to 'Kynaston's Cave/Viewpoint'. Ignore the first flight of steps but walk along a level path on the edge of the woods.

② At a signpost with orange and green arrows, turn left up a flight of steps; the signpost arm says 'Kynaston's Cave'. At the top of the steps you come to a flat area where there is a second information board. The cave is cut into the rock face at the top of a flight of steps. Turn right now and walk along with the rock face on your left. The path soon starts to climb, with a fence on the right to bring you to the top of the hill.

③ Go straight ahead with a new fence now on your left and pine trees all around. Where the fence ends go ahead on a narrow path between rhododendron bushes. This path emerges into a clearing with two picnic tables and a signpost beyond them. This signpost has an arm without any writing on it, but go ahead in the direction indicated, again a narrow path

Looking towards the Breidden Hills

through rhododendron bushes and up a short slope to emerge at the viewpoint.

④ Turn right. Follow a level path away from the viewpoint; this soon begins to descend and passes through the banks of the Iron Age fort where you will find a third information board. Continue on the now wide track which ends by farm buildings.

⑤ Turn left then right at a signpost, 'Kynaston's Cave', and follow a wide, level track which soon bears to the right. At a T junction by a pond, turn left and follow this track as it descends, ignoring the next signpost to the cave.

⑥ Turn right on a wide, sandy track which runs along the edge of the hill with a field on the other side. This takes you back to the start.

PLACES OF INTEREST NEARBY

Merrington Green Nature Reserve – 8 miles east of Nesscliffe (GR 465210) – a remnant of medieval common extending to 12 hectares, including woodland, scrub, grassland and several ponds, all rich in wildlife. It is in the care of Shropshire Wildlife Trust and is always open. Car park. Telephone 01743 241691.

Tibberton
The Sutherland Arms

MAP: OS EXPLORER 243 (GR 681205)   WALK 10   **DISTANCE:** 3 MILES

DIRECTIONS TO START: TIBBERTON IS 3 MILES WEST OF NEWPORT. FROM SHREWSBURY OR NEWPORT TAKE THE B5062. TURN OFF WHEN SIGNPOSTED 'TIBBERTON', WHICH IS 1 MILE NORTH OF THE B ROAD. **PARKING:** IN THE PUB CAR PARK, WITH PERMISSION.

In his poem *A Shropshire Lad*, A.E. Housman writes about the 'blue remembered hills' and these words came to me on the return stretch. In the distance the Wrekin can be seen with its attendant foothills. In settled weather with still air, these hills do indeed look blue. Caynton Mill, halfway round the walk, is quite delightful, situated alongside the River Meese with its overhanging willows and beds of trailing reeds. Do look over the bridge opposite the mill – could a scene be more idyllic? At the side of the mill is the millrace and signs of the wheel which it turned. This is a lovely walk, level throughout and so peaceful with only the songs of the birds disturbing the tranquillity. Although close to Newport and the conurbation of Telford, neither of these impinge on the sheer delight of this part of rural Shropshire.

The Sutherland Arms

Originally built some 300 years ago as a farmhouse and inn, the Sutherland Arms still has the feel of a private residence. The bar is placed four square in the middle with the rooms grouped around it so that it serves all sides. There is a welcoming 'public bar', as well as a comfortable lounge with brocade wall seats and canal paintings, and a dining room. Outside on the patio, summer days see many attractive blue and white picnic tables under a large awning. An excellent and varied menu offers ploughman's, baguettes, jacket potatoes, salads and burgers as well as an all-day breakfast, plus a good selection of fish and meat dishes. In addition there is a specials board which always includes vegetarian meals – and children are not forgotten either. Draught ales include Bank's Mild and Bitter and Marston's Pedigree; Extra Cold Guinness is on tap and there are several lagers and, for cider drinkers, Bulmer's Original. Opening times are Monday to Friday 12 noon to 2.30 pm and 5 pm to 11 pm (but from 6 pm Monday and Tuesday). Saturday hours are 11 am to 11 pm and Sunday 12 noon to 10.30 pm (not Monday evening). Telephone: 01952 550533.

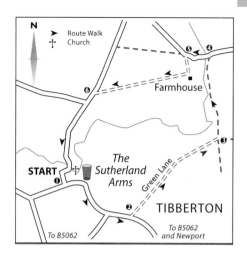

The Walk

① From the pub turn left and walk out of the village.

② Just after passing Yew Tree Farm, on the opposite side of the road, turn left onto a wide level track marked with a 'Bridleway' signpost. Soon you pass between two ponds. The fields on either side are large but fringed with trees and with the woods beyond give an air of serenity.

③ You come to a junction of tracks. Turn left, still on the same track but with more grass and fringed with nettles for a short distance in summer, but not so as to get in the way as the path is still very wide. Passing a small copse on the left, which is alive with snowdrops and bluebells in spring, cross a drainage ditch by an unseen bridge and enter a field. Continue ahead with a fence on the right and soon enter a narrow stretch with the river on your left and a field on your right. The grassy track emerges into the field behind the mill and continues ahead along the side of the field to the lane.

④ Turn left in the lane to Caynton Mill. The millrace is on the left and the gardens over the bridge on the right should not be missed. Walk on along the lane as far as Wood Cottage.

⑤ Turn left onto a farm track. Follow this

The delightful gardens at Caynton Mill

for 100 yards, then, by trees near Wood Farm, you turn right onto a second track which runs, straight as a die, to join the lane at Pine Ridge. This is a private path and used with the kind permission of the owner at Bank House Farm so do please keep to the track and leave no litter.

(6) At the lane turn left and, passing Bank House Farm, return to the pub. On reaching Tibberton do pause to look over the bridge at a second millrace. The mill, a paper mill which closed in 1932, has now been replaced by a house but the scene from the bridge, with the church dominating, hasn't changed.

PLACES OF INTEREST NEARBY

Weston Park, 6 miles south-east of Newport (GR 800108) on the A5, is the home of the Earl of Bradford and, as well as the house, park and gardens, includes a deer park, a woodland adventure playground for children, and a miniature railway. Special events take place throughout the year. Telephone: 01952 852100.

Uffington
The Corbet Arms

MAP: OS EXPLORER 241 (GR 528138)   WALK 11   **DISTANCE:** 2¾ MILES

DIRECTIONS TO START: UFFINGTON IS 3 MILES NORTH-EAST OF SHREWSBURY. FROM THE TOWN, USE THE B5062 NEWPORT ROAD AND TURN RIGHT AFTER THE BYPASS, OR THE B4380 AND TURN LEFT AT ATCHAM. **PARKING:** IN THE PUB'S LARGE CAR PARK, BUT PLEASE INFORM THE LANDLORD.

A most enjoyable walk this and although it does involve one short, steep climb, the views are well worth the effort. Haughmond Hill, a sandstone island in the North Shropshire plain, capped with pines and birch, looks out over the Severn Vale to the south Shropshire hills and Wales. It is a very popular viewpoint, giving many opportunities for people to just 'stand and stare'. In spring the wooded slopes are alive with wildflowers. Uffington is today a small village but once it was an important and bustling port on the canal system that linked Shrewsbury with the main inland waterways. A ferry, operated from just behind the church and worked by an overhead cable, formerly plied its trade across the river for pedestrians to get into town. This lovely little circuit offers you merely a sample of the hill's delights – there are a myriad paths to be explored on another visit.

The Corbet Arms

The Corbets date back to the time of William the Conqueror and beyond, and descendants of the family still farm in Shropshire. The haunted Corbet Arms is one of their former homes and has been a public house for about 100 years, catering at first for passing cyclists. The already large non-smoking and very comfortable dining area with its long blue seats has been extended and now includes a conservatory with superb views south across the river to Shrewsbury and the south Shropshire hills – try to get a window seat if you can. China plates and paintings of country scenes decorate the walls while in the public bar (no children in here) you will find collections of cigarette cards. Outside, around the bowling green, which adds to the enjoyment of the view, there are more tables where meals can be taken in suitable weather. A very extensive main menu of meat and fish dishes plus a specials board will have something for everyone and in addition to snacks such as jacket potatoes there is also a children's menu. Greenalls Mild and a guest beer are always on offer, as well as Guinness and Strongbow cider. The opening hours are 12 noon to 3 pm and 7 pm to 11 pm (10.30 pm on Sundays). Food is available every day (except Monday lunchtime) from 12 noon to 2 pm and 7 pm to 9.30 pm (9 pm on Sunday and Monday evenings). Telephone: 01743 709232.

The Walk

① From the car park turn right and walk south out of the village. Bear left onto a minor lane, signposted 'Upton Magna'.

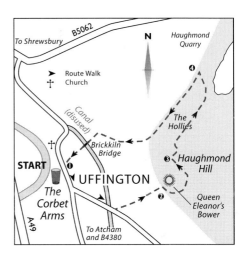

After ¼ mile turn left through a gap where a gate ought to be and walk towards the hill along the side of the left-hand field, that is with the hedge on your right. At the stile at the foot of the hill turn right.

② In just a few yards fork left at a waymark post up a narrow track, leaving the fields behind you; the track becomes fairly steep. At the top turn left at another waymark post and, passing a half-dead Scots pine, reach the main viewpoint – a bare outcrop of rock on a wide grassy plateau marked by another Scots pine. You are now looking south to the Shropshire hill country, Wenlock Edge, the Stretton Hills and Stiperstones, while to the right you can see the Breiddens and the Welsh mountains and to the extreme right Grinshall and Nesscliffe.

③ With your back to the view walk across the open area to join a wide track coming from the right and head for a gate just visible ahead; here turn left, keeping outside the broken fence. The fence, which is always close by on your right, soon turns

Haughmond Hill

right and you follow it for ¼ mile. Eventually you will come to where two paths fork, near which, over the fence, is a sign 'Keep Out Quarry Workings'. Fork left downhill and in just a few yards you will be able to see, below you through the trees, the lower track.

④ Turn left along the track. At the end of the field on your right the track bends right into a wide avenue of trees and brambles. Follow this until you come to a giant electricity pylon. Right underneath it turn left to a stile on the edge of the avenue. Cross

the stile and go slightly right to cross the canal by an old packhorse bridge. Now go ahead to the village and you will find the pub straight in front when you reach the road.

PLACES OF INTEREST NEARBY

Attingham House and Park (National Trust) is just south of Uffington, across the A5. This fine country mansion, built in 1783 from Grinshall stone by the first Lord Berwick, is noted for its fine Regency interior and landscaped grounds. The park is open from dawn to dusk every day, except Christmas Day; the house from Easter to October (not Wednesday or Thursday). Telephone: 01743 708123.

Pontesbury
The Nag's Head

MAP: OS EXPLORER 241 (GR 409062) | **WALK 12** | DISTANCE: 2¼ MILES

DIRECTIONS TO START: PONTESBURY IS 7 MILES SOUTH-WEST OF SHREWSBURY ON THE A488 ROAD TO BISHOP'S CASTLE. THE INN IS ON YOUR RIGHT AS YOU COME INTO THE VILLAGE FROM THE EAST. **PARKING:** IN THE PUB CAR PARK, WITH PERMISSION.

Through some of Shropshire's most beautiful countryside this stroll is a delight throughout. It is a route for all seasons, being on either quiet country lanes or along dry stony tracks. Part of the walk traverses the Shropshire Wildlife Trust's land of Earl's Hill, which, together with Pontesford Hill, is rather reminiscent of a crouching lion when viewed from afar. This circuit keeps you on the lower slopes of the hill with no steep climbs of any kind, but if you wish to go to the top the ascent from point 4 is fairly gradual and easy to follow. The views are well worth the effort! There are, however, some lovely views from the walk itself. Pontesbury has grown in recent years as a dormitory town for Shrewsbury but the area around the church has some original buildings of architectural interest. The village's claim to fame is of being the home of the novelist Mary Webb.

The Nag's Head

A very warm welcome awaits you in this recently renovated pub. The bar has an open fireplace and beamed ceiling and is probably the oldest part. Separated is a small lounge, comfortably furnished with easy chairs, and beyond there is a non-smoking dining room with a relaxed atmosphere. Outside is a good sized garden with tables, and a children's play area. A vast menu is on offer, including a variety of fish and meat dishes, vegetarian and children's meals, ploughman's and baguettes, and the traditional Sunday roast. The ales are Morland's Old Speckled Hen, Tetley's and a guest beer, plus Carling lager and Strongbow cider. The Nag's Head is open all day on Friday, Saturday and Sunday, and keeps the usual opening hours on Monday to Thursday. Food is available at all reasonable times. Telephone: 01743 791697.

The Walk

① Cross the road and turn along Bogey Lane, almost opposite. Pass the school buildings and, at the road junction opposite the library, turn left. At the end of Linley Terrace, turn left again.

② Turn left by the letter box and walk up Grove Lane towards the hill. Go straight on at the next road junction, walking along the lane marked with a no through road sign. Pass a cottage called 'Callow' and then the road becomes a stony track.

③ You come to a junction of tracks. Ignore the bridleway sign on the corner just in front of you; instead, turn left and go to the gate a few yards away. Go through the

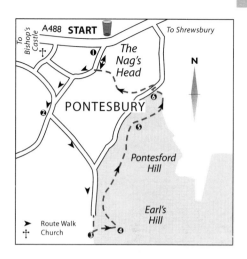

kissing a gate and walk ahead on a brown bare earth track.

④ The bare brown track turns to green grass and when it does look out for the waymark post on your left with a green arrow on it. If you want to go to the top of the hill go straight on – you will find a fairly easy but steep path ahead – otherwise turn left and cross the stile. You now walk along the west side of the hill on a level track. At first narrow, it soon widens, wide enough for a horse and cart in times long gone.

⑤ Ignore a footpath joining on your left but keep straight on. The path narrows a little but then widens again just before the viewpoint. Don't miss this. It is an Iron Age fort established in 600 BC and the views are quite dramatic and well worth stopping for. Turning your back on the viewpoint, return to the track and go left downhill.

⑥ On reaching the lane turn right down the hill and at the bottom turn left onto a

Pontesbury village

stony track and cross the cattle grid. Cross the next cattle grid by a house and fork right, diagonally, across a field, heading towards the school, to a stile visible in the far corner. On reaching the tarmac track, turn right. At the lane by the school turn right to return to the pub.

PLACES OF INTEREST NEARBY

Mitchell's Fold, 9 miles south-west (GR 304983). Two miles beyond Hope village, turn right off the A488 by an old restored mine building. This is a mysterious stone circle some 75 feet in diameter with 15 surviving upright stones and is a lovely area for walking or a picnic – splendid views. Always open.

Ryton
The Fox

DIRECTIONS TO START: TAKE THE A49 TO DORRINGTON, 5 MILES SOUTH OF SHREWSBURY. TURN LEFT THERE, SIGNPOSTED 'RYTON'. IN RYTON TURN RIGHT. THE FOX IS THE LAST BUILDING AT THE FAR END OF THE VILLAGE. **PARKING:** IN THE PUB CAR PARK, WITH PERMISSION.

Ryton is just a collection of a few houses and farms lining the quiet lanes which link the two parts – Great and Little – separated as they are by a field. The local economy is based firmly on agriculture, and this is a level walk through glorious countryside with views south to the Stretton Hills. After a short stroll south along a lane, the route turns east to cross a couple of fields and it is from here that some of the best views are to be found, with Caer Caradoc in the distance. The walk then turns north along a farm track to pass the village hall and another part of the village, which includes the one large house, Ryton Grove, before continuing along a track with more views to the distant hills. We then return to the Fox in Little Ryton by way of some more back lanes.

The Fox

It is not often one finds such a delightful pub so far off the beaten track, but the location of the Fox takes a lot of beating. From the much coveted bay windows one gets an uninterrupted view south to the Stretton Hills – little wonder these are the first tables to be snapped up so if you want a delightful view while enjoying your meal book a dining room bay window in advance. The dining room is a non-smoking area. On a sunny day there are a few tables on the patio out front where you can enjoy the view and an outdoor meal. To survive, a pub so remote has to have a good reputation for food, and that is certainly the case here. The lunchtime bar meals, 12 noon to 2.30 pm, are of plain English cooking, including fish and chips, steak and ale pie, ploughman's, baguettes and jacket potatoes, while the evening menu, from 7 pm, is of a more oriental or Mediterranean character; all meals are freshly prepared and use local produce where possible. Vegetarians are catered for and there are half portions for children. The real ales on offer include Hobsons Best Bitter, Buckley's Reverend James, Worthington Best and Banks's Bitter plus two guest beers from local breweries and there is also Scrumpy Jack cider. The Fox is open daily from 12 noon to 3 pm and 7 pm to 11 pm (10.30 pm Sunday). It is closed Monday lunchtimes. Telephone: 01743 718499.

The Walk

① Turn right out of the car park and walk along the lane. Ignore any footpath signs on the right. One hundred yards after

passing Holywell Farm on the right, look for a stile on the left marked by a footpath signpost; there is another footpath sign and stile opposite on the other side of the lane.

② Turn left over the stile and walk ahead with the hedge on your right. It is from here that you get the best views to the south; Lawley is the nearest hill and further south is Caer Caradoc, reputed to be where Caractacus, a British chieftan, made his last stand against the invading Romans. Cross the next waymarked stile and continue ahead, still by the hedge. Just after a kink in the hedge is a field gate; cross the waymarked stile alongside it and continue in the same direction as before but now with the hedge on your left. Cross the last stile by another field gate.

③ Turn left in a green lane and, if there is mud here, keep to the left. The track soon becomes dry and, eventually, joins a metalled lane by a former farmhouse called 'The Hollies', the name of which is not shown. Continue ahead now on the metalled lane until you come to some

The two hills, Lawley and Caer Caradoc

houses on the eastern edge of the village. Pass the village hall on your right and continue ahead. The lane bends to the right at Ryton Farm Holiday Cottages and then bends to the left.

④ At a second right-hand bend go straight ahead on to a level hard, dry track which skirts the back of the farm buildings and wends its way dead ahead between two open fields for ¼ mile.

⑤ On reaching the next lane turn left and at the next road junction turn left again, signposted 'Ryton ¼'. Walk along this lane for only 100 yards and then you fork left again, still signposted 'Ryton'. This new lane is much quieter and takes you back through the hamlet, past the letterbox and out again. The pub is now straight ahead.

> **PLACES OF INTEREST NEARBY**
> **Acton Burnell Castle and Langley Chapel** – 3 miles east. The castle, now a shell with nicely tended grounds, is the site of the first ever English Parliament in 1283. Langley Chapel was built in 1564 and is still preserved as it was then. Both are in the care of English Heritage and are always open.

Cressage
The Eagles

MAP: OS EXPLORER 241 (GR 592042)　　**WALK 14**　　**DISTANCE:** 2½ MILES

DIRECTIONS TO START: CRESSAGE IS SOUTH-EAST OF SHREWSBURY ON THE A458 TO MUCH WENLOCK. THE EAGLES IS ON THE MAIN ROAD. **PARKING:** YOU ARE WELCOME TO USE THE PUB CAR PARK, ALL THE VILLAGERS DO!

Wide views over the Severn Valley are the hallmark of this walk. Cressage is situated on high ground overlooking the flood plain of the river below. This is a pleasant stroll along two quiet country lanes with just the tinkling of the stream for company. An easy footpath, which crosses three fields, links the lanes. The best views are obtained from the second of these fields from where you have the Wrekin, the most easterly of the South Shropshire hills, dominating the view northwards. Cressage is an ancient village and owes its existence originally to being the nearest habitable place to a ford across the Severn, now replaced by a bridge. Later it had a Norman motte. It has grown in recent times, with new housing developments carefully placed behind the older part of the village. The name Cressage is derived from Cristesac, a Saxon name meaning Christ's Oak, and it is believed to be the only village with such a name. The oak once grew where the war memorial now stands, on the bend just in front of the pub. It was here, so tradition has it, that St Augustine, an emissary from the Pope, preached to the Welsh bishops in AD 584.

The Eagles

This comfortable, welcoming 17th century coaching inn has three rooms – the main public bar and the lounge bar with a separate non-smoking dining area, the two linked by a huge fireplace accessible from either side. On a sunny day the light streams in through the lattice windows of the dining section – a very pleasant place to eat. The lounge bar is dominated by the countless brasses, brass pots, jugs and cooking utensils of every kind which hang from the thick oak beams and cover the walls, while in the corner is a large fish tank. Outside are two garden areas with tables, also a children's play area. The menu has sufficient variety to suit everyone: soup, many meat dishes, fish, broccoli and cheese bake, sandwiches and baguettes. There is also a specials board. Beers include Greenalls Mild, Courage Directors and Carling lager, as well as Strongbow and Woodpecker cider. The Eagles is open all day from 11 am, with food available from 12 noon to 3 pm and 6.30 pm to 9.30 pm – and ice creams at any time of day. Telephone: 01952 510303.

The Walk

① Turn left from the main car entrance at the pub and head south towards the church. There is a pavement all the way until you have to cross the road when you reach the first lane on the right, signposted 'Harnage and Kenley'.

② Walk along the lane for ³/₄ mile. Ignore the first footpath you come to, with a public footpath signpost, just beyond the

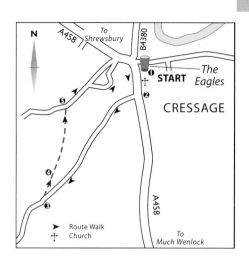

last cottage on the edge of the village; continue along the lane until you come to a second stile, also with a public footpath signpost.

③ Cross the stile into a field with bracken in this corner. The tiny stream is crossed by a footbridge a little way to the right but the stream is so narrow that it's easy enough just to step over it anywhere. With the hedge on your left, walk up the slope. There is a footbridge in the hollow ahead but it is hidden at first, so make your way towards the treeline, slowly moving further away from the hedge. The footbridge is nearer the right-hand corner than it is to the left-hand corner.

④ Cross the footbridge and continue ahead, straight up the field to the left of the wooden electricity pole. On reaching the top of the slope you will see a field gate and a stile alongside it. Cross the stile and bear slightly right as waymarked, aiming for a point about 50 yards left of the red brick house to reach a stile.

The wonderful view which awaits at the end of the walk

⑤ Turn right down the lane and, having passed the house, fork right onto a green lane. Shortly, on your left, you will see a pair of delightful Tudor-style houses, which, I understand, was once a public house but is now in private ownership. The track wends its way round to emerge onto the main road. Cross the road to the pavement opposite and turn right to return to the start, passing, as you do so, the village war memorial.

PLACES OF INTEREST NEARBY

Buildwas Abbey – a few miles west of Cressage via the B4380. A delightful ruined Cistercian abbey, in the care of English Heritage, set beside the River Severn against a backdrop of wooded grounds; a very pleasant place to amble round on a sunny day. Open April to September daily from 11 am to 5 pm. Telephone: 01952 433274.

Ironbridge
The Tontine Hotel

MAP: OS EXPLORER 242 (GR 672034) | **WALK 15** | DISTANCE: 3½ MILES

DIRECTIONS TO START: TAKE THE A4169 MUCH WENLOCK-TELFORD ROAD. AT BUILDWAS TURN EAST ON THE B4380. PAST THE IRON BRIDGE, FORK RIGHT, THEN TURN RIGHT. FOLLOW SIGN FOR B4372 BROSLEY ACROSS JACKFIELD BRIDGE, AND AT THE HAIRPIN BEND GO AHEAD, SIGNED 'IRON BRIDGE P'. **PARKING:** USE THE PAY AND DISPLAY CAR PARK AT THE IRON BRIDGE. THE PUB IS ON THE OTHER SIDE OF THE BRIDGE.

I love this walk through the woods of Benthall Edge with its wildflowers and birds. Apart from easy-to-avoid puddles on the trackbed of the former railway it's dry all the way, and the views – well, you are in for a real treat. At one point you suddenly emerge from the trees on the edge of a field with a great view north; there is the Wrekin towering over the valley and Buildwas Abbey like a toy fort down by the river. Then, along the track past Benthall Hall Farm, views open up to the north and south. Benthall church is a most attractive place and as you cross the fields you get a full frontal view of Benthall Hall. The climb through the woods is long but gentle; otherwise the walk is mostly level, and it is fully waymarked throughout.

The Tontine Hotel

On a riverside site right by the famous Iron Bridge, the fascinating Tontine Hotel, built in the 18th century, opened as a pub in 1784. The exterior has changed little since the days of the Industrial Revolution. Its spacious interior is a perfect example of the Victorian style, and all the décor is typical of the period. At one end is an open fireplace of cast iron with a surround of tiles, locally made, as indeed are the floor tiles in the entrance hall. The walls bear many engravings of Ironbridge past. The bars are very comfortable and the vast and comprehensive menu contains something for everyone, including children, with light bites such as ploughman's, sandwiches and jacket potatoes as well as vegetarian dishes. The beers on offer are Banks's and M&B Brew XI, alongside Carling lager and Woodpecker cider. Overnight accommodation is also available. The pub is open all day from 11 am, with meals served from 12 noon to 3 pm and 6 pm to 9 pm. Telephone: 01952 432127, website www.tontine-ironbridge.co.uk

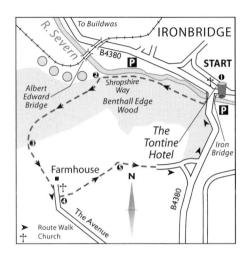

The Walk

① From the pub cross the bridge and turn right at the car park to walk along the trackbed of the former GWR railway line from Bridgnorth to Shrewsbury, the rails of which can still be seen in the roadway.

② At the power station cooling towers, turn left through the gate then left again up the embankment to a junction of tracks marked by a signpost. Here there is a seat for weary walkers to rest awhile. Fork right to take the sunken track, signposted 'Benthall'. This track climbs steadily for ¹/₂ mile and gives you fantastic views from the gaps in the trees.

③ A wide dirt track joins here, coming steeply up from your right; follow it as it bends round to the left and shortly right again to meet, at a gate and stile, a level stony track heading towards Benthall Farm house. Along this track you get the best views to the west and east. Pass the farm and its immaculate brick barns, which must be of considerable age, and then the churchyard extension, on the right, and the church and the older churchyard, on the left.

④ By the church, as you join a metalled lane, go through the little wicket gate at the side of the older churchyard and strike out across the field on a well-tended grassy path. Here you get a good view of the front of Benthall Hall. The hall belongs to the National Trust and is open on Wednesdays and Saturdays from Easter to September. Go through the gateway on the other side

The Ironbridge and the River Avon

of the field by a kissing gate and continue ahead along the side of the field with the hedge on your left.

⑤ Join a grassy lane and turn right. This winds its way between fields and a wood to become a lane after the farm and drops down to a junction with a minor road where it says 'Spout Lane'. Now turn left downhill. Near the bottom of the hill the pavement and road part company and you descend in a straight line down a few steps to the car park.

PLACES OF INTEREST NEARBY

Ironbridge Gorge has no less than nine museums, of which Blists Hill is the most famous. Special events in costume add to the atmosphere of a real working Victorian town. Visit also **Benthall Hall**, which you pass on the walk. Contact the tourist information centre (three doors down from the Tontine), telephone: 01952 432166, website www.ironbridge.org.uk

Chirbury
The Herbert Arms Hotel

DIRECTIONS TO START: CHIRBURY IS 21 MILES SOUTH-WEST OF SHREWSBURY ON THE B4386 AND 6 MILES SOUTH OF WELSHPOOL ON THE A490. **PARKING:** PATRONS ARE WELCOME TO USE THE HOTEL CAR PARK WHILE WALKING.

A perfect walk across fields while all around is wide open country. The route takes you past an old mill in a pretty wooded valley and through deciduous woods. Chirbury stands on high ground above the vale of the River Severn on the border of England and Wales, its village street made very attractive by the many half-timbered and stone cottages. The church is built on the site of an Augustinian priory of 13th century origin, and part of the Chapter House can still be found in the far left corner of the churchyard. Beyond the churchyard is Chirbury Hall Farm; when Henry VIII dissolved the monasteries stone from the priory was used in its construction. The River Camlad, which is crossed on the walk, is unique in being the only river that flows from England into Wales, where it joins up with the River Severn.

The Herbert Arms Hotel

The pub, which stands next door to the church, dates from the early part of the 18th century. Originally called the Cross, it was once a coaching inn, being on the main road from Welshpool to Bishop's Castle and Ludlow. The single-storey extension on the right, now the main dining area, was formerly the stables. The Royal Regiment of Wales was actually formed in this building although we are in England! Bed and breakfast accommodation is available and the resident ghost, who rattles cups and saucers, is an added attraction at no extra charge! The Herbert Arms offers a take-away service in addition to its bar meals, which can be enjoyed in the extremely comfortable lounge with its lush green settles and oak-beamed ceiling. A small garden has tables for outside meals in summer. The extensive menu includes many fish and meat dishes as well as vegetarian food and the traditional Sunday lunch, and the pub is noted for its home-made curries. There is also a speciality of the day, such as pheasant. Beers include M&B Mild, Worthington draught, Murphy's and Grolsch lager, also Strongbow and Woodpecker cider on draught. The opening hours are 12 noon to 3 pm and 7 pm to 10 pm, with food available throughout. Telephone: 01938 561216.

The Walk

① From the pub turn right through the churchyard and right again at the school onto a tarmac footpath. Cross the main road and turn left. About 50 yards after the footpath ends, and just beyond the word

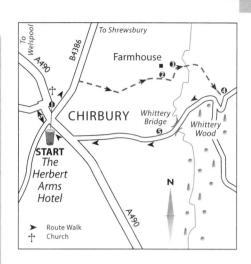

'Slow' painted on the road, look for a stile. Cross this and head up the field with the hedge on your right. Cross the next stile and continue ahead to another stile silhouetted on the skyline and here bear left across a big field, heading just to the right of the Heightley farmhouse.

② Near the farm head for the double wooden pylon ahead. Below you is the old ruin of Heightley Mill, a former flour mill. Cross a stile and bear left, dropping down the slope as indicated at any convenient point. It's best to keep to the left of the scrub hedge and gently make your way down the slope to the track at the end.

③ At the farm track turn right, cross the bridge and bear right as waymarked up a short slope into a flat grassy area. Bear right again to pass a second waymark post and go up a short slope between bushes of gorse. At the top by the wooden pylon find a gate in the corner, go through and walk along the edge of the woods until you come to another stile and the lane.

View of Chirbury from the path

④ At the lane turn right and follow it downhill. Just before Whittery Bridge over the River Camlad, on your right is a track, only a short track now which ends in a field just round the corner, but in the 19th century this was the main track which the carts used to carry wheat to the flour mill at Heightley.

⑤ Cross the bridge and walk back along the quiet lane to the village. There are very pleasant views ahead when you reach the top of the road. Turn right at the main road but only for a short way as you soon reach the village. Continue ahead, passing the post office to return to the start.

PLACES OF INTEREST NEARBY

Powis Castle (National Trust) just south-west of Welshpool (GR 215063). The world-famous gardens feature enormous clipped yews laid out in French and Italian styles. The medieval castle, which is perched above the Severn Vale, has a fine collection of paintings and furniture. Open Easter to October (closed on Mondays, also Tuesday except July/August). Telephone: 01938 557018.

Stiperstones
The Stiperstones Inn

MAP: OS EXPLORER 216 (GR 363004)   **WALK 17**   **DISTANCE:** 2¼ MILES

DIRECTIONS TO START: STIPERSTONES VILLAGE IS 12 MILES SOUTH-WEST OF SHREWSBURY. TURN SOUTH-EAST OFF THE A488 BISHOP'S CASTLE ROAD AT PLOXGREEN WHICH IS 2 MILES SOUTH OF MINSTERLEY. **PARKING:** PATRONS ARE WELCOME TO USE THE PUB'S LARGE CAR PARK WHILE WALKING.

This charming but remote part of Shropshire, now so green and quiet, was once the heart of an industrial area with lead and baryte mines and great chimneys belching out smoke on every side, and this activity with its attendant infrastructure of mineral railways and overhead bucket lines stretched from Snailbeach in the north to The Bog in the south. Now all that has vanished, leaving a green and peaceful countryside, ideal for a quiet walk. Many other guidebooks take the walker up onto the Stiperstones mountain itself so, by way of contrast, this route stays in the valley to give a pleasant and easy stroll through woods and fields with great views – all especially enriched in July/August when the mountain is alive with the purple of heather. The walk is mainly level with one very short climb.

The Stiperstones Inn

This 300 year old building with its walls of white stucco is situated in the heart of the village and now encompasses the village shop, post office and tourist information centre in what was formerly part farmhouse and part mine. The lounge, with its oak beams and brasses, is cosy and very comfortable, with long leather settles along each side and an open fireplace, while there is also a dining area and a public bar as well. Outside, trees and the slopes of the mountain, which reach down to the very village, shelter several tables where meals can be taken in summer and horses in the paddock keep the children amused. The good selection of beers on offer includes Boddingtons Bitter, Highgate Special and Dark Mild, also Heineken lager and two ciders, Strongbow and Woodpecker. The excellent menu of starters, main dishes, sweets and bar snacks such as ploughman's will ensure you don't go hungry. Overnight accommodation is also available. The opening hours are from 7.30 am until 11 pm and food is available all day, 7.30 am to 10 pm and includes breakfasts. Telephone: 01743 791327, website www.stiperstones.co.uk

The Walk

① From the pub turn right and walk along the road for 100 yards. Just before the yellow stripes on the road fork left by a house called 'Conifers' and go down a short slope. Now follow the farm track past Hogstow Farm and on the bend where the track swings right towards Whitebanks Farm go through the facing gate, leaving

the farm track. Now walk up the side of the field on a fenced off bridleway, fence on the left and a hedge on the right; this track bears left into the woods and climbs gently to a field gate.

② Go through the gate and follow the ridge path, passing the first of several waymark posts and ignoring the bridleway branching off to the right. In a little while at a second waymark post the track, as signed, forks left down a short slope to run alongside the fields with lovely views across the valley to the village and the mountain. The Devil's Chair is the largest outcrop of rocks above the village. Pass the end of the woods and cross an open field, heading straight for the chimney of Tankerville Mine, now a museum.

③ Turn left along the farm track and join the road; from here there is a superb view across the Shropshire plain. Pass the letterbox and walk down the road as far as the first bend. Cross the road and go over the the stile by the forest gate. Walk up through the woods to the stile at the top.

The view over the Shropshire plain

④ Turn left over the stile and walk along by the fence for 50 yards to a second stile. Cross this and bear slightly right to walk down a long sloping field close to the outer boundary of the woods. In the bottom left-hand corner of the field, cross the last stile and descend to the road again along a short narrow path. Turn right to return to the pub.

PLACES OF INTEREST NEARBY

Snailbeach – formerly the centre of the local mining industry. There are many restored mining buildings, mineral railway remains and artefacts, also several colour-coded walks from the village hall. Some mine workings are opened from time to time. Ask at the pub for information or telephone: 01742 791360.

Bridges
The Horse Shoe Inn

MAP: OS EXPLORER 217 (GR 394965)   ·   WALK 18   ·   **DISTANCE:** 1½, 2 OR 2¼ MILES

DIRECTIONS TO START: BRIDGES IS 14 MILES SOUTH-WEST OF SHREWSBURY ON AN UNCLASSIFIED ROAD TO BISHOP'S CASTLE AND 4 MILES WEST OF CHURCH STRETTON, WHICH IS CONNECTED TO BRIDGES BY A MOUNTAIN ROAD. THE INN IS JUST OFF THE MAIN ROAD; LOOK OUT FOR ITS SIGN AT THE JUNCTION JUST ABOVE IT.
PARKING: THERE IS A PUBLIC CAR PARK OPPOSITE THE INN.

The vale of the River East Onny is wide and undulating; this is sheep country par excellence with hills all around. The walk follows the Shropshire Way for a mile and enjoys superb views from short-cropped grassy fields, returning along quiet country lanes. Bridges is just a small hamlet of a few scattered houses and farmsteads and so called on account of the many bridges found in the area – we shall see or cross most of them.

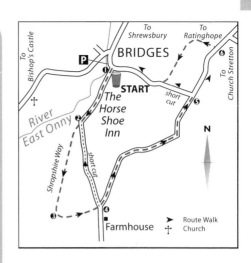

The Horse Shoe Inn

The Horse Shoe dates from the 14th century and was originally a coaching inn. Today, in spite of its remote situation, its reputation for food and comfort has spread and people come from far and wide. In summer the inn's south-facing aspect is a veritable suntrap and the tables at the front as well as on the wide lawn alongside the running water of Darnford Brook allow you to eat outside in very pleasant surroundings. The interior is large and comfortable with an open fireplace and low-beamed ceilings. There is a vast choice of food, from the exotic to the everyday, with extras on the blackboard and hefty sandwiches. The pub is noted for its collection of ales and ciders: Shepherd Neame Spitfire comes from Kent and Adnams Bitter from Suffolk; others include Timothy Taylor Landlord, while for the cider drinker there is Weston's Old Rosie and Stowford Press. The pub is open all day from 11 am. Food is served on weekdays from 12 noon to 3 pm and 6 pm to 9 pm, and all day at weekends. A holiday flat is also available. Telephone: 01588 650260.

The Walk

① Turn left from the pub, crossing the first of several bridges on this walk, and go up the lane for ¹/₂ mile. Now fork right at the footpath signpost 'Shropshire Way and Adstone Walk', onto the level grassy track.

② Go through the gate on the left and head uphill alongside a line of trees; the way is marked by the Shropshire Way's buzzard sign, the tip of the beak pointing

to the line of the path. Follow the fence and row of beech trees to the top of the field then head towards a small copse of larches growing on the hillside. On your right is the vale of the River East Onny and, as you leave the beech trees behind, on your left and slightly behind, you will have a lovely view of the Upper Darnford Valley. Keep to the right of the larches. As you near the top of the field the Long Mynd can be seen away to the south-east.

③ With Coates Farm below, turn left to a field gate, beyond which is a track leading down to the farm.

④ If you wish to cut the walk short, turn hard left at the first barn and follow the lane downhill to point 2. Otherwise, with Coates Farm on your right, go ahead on to the lane which skirts the top of the open field. From here you can look down on Overs Farm and probably be able to see ostriches in the fields.

⑤ Just before the road junction you can see the second of the bridges below to your

One of the many superb views seen on the way

left. At the junction you again have a choice of shortening the walk by following the lane down to the left, but we will continue ahead to Ratlinghope.

⑥ Opposite the Manor House turn left over the stile by the public footpath signposted 'Darnford Walk', and go down the field to cross the stream by the third bridge. Turn left and follow the track with the stream on your left through some very pleasant woods. At the road cross the stile and turn right. On reaching the pub again you will see a footbridge – that makes four

– and if you walk through the car park on the right of it you will just fail to see a fifth bridge because of the undergrowth.

PLACES OF INTEREST NEARBY

The Long Mynd is an upland area of some 6,000 acres of heather and bracken. Very popular with walkers, riders and bird watchers, it is easily accessible by car and has many parking areas. Information from the pub, the National Trust (telephone: 01694 723068) or the tourist information centre (telephone: 01694 723133 (Easter– October) or 722535).

All Stretton
The Yew Tree

MAP: OS EXPLORER 217 (GR 460955)   **WALK 19**   **DISTANCE:** 1¾ MILES

DIRECTIONS TO START: ALL STRETTON IS 13 MILES SOUTH OF SHREWSBURY. DRIVE DOWN THE A49 AND FORK RIGHT AT THE SIGNPOST FOR CARDINGMILL VALLEY. ALL STRETTON IS THE FIRST VILLAGE YOU COME TO AND THE YEW TREE IS ON THE RIGHT. **PARKING:** IN THE PUB CAR PARK, WITH PERMISSION.

The Long Mynd is the principal attraction for walkers in south Shropshire and this stroll should whet your appetite to explore it further. By using very attractive and non strenuous paths, I hope it will encourage you to do more walking in this lovely area. After an easy, level start, a short climb before Cwmdale takes you through a pass to the delightful main valley, Batch Valley, one of many on this eastern side of the hill.

Situated on the flat lands between the Long Mynd to the west and Caer Caradoc to the east, the hamlet of All Stretton is a delightful spot. The slopes of the Long Mynd come right down to the edge of the village, many of whose houses are built of stone hewn from the hill itself. All Stretton is just a mile from Church Stretton, the main market town in the area and a great centre for walkers wishing to explore the hills.

The Yew Tree

This pub, now the only survivor of five once found in the village, dates back to 1620. It took its name from a yew tree, which, sadly, was felled in the 1990s when it was found to be unsafe. There is a large garden at the back with outdoor tables, ideal on a warm summer day, and a play area for children is also provided. The lounge bar is the main dining area and very comfortable it is with its brocade settles and wall to wall carpet. The beamed ceiling, open fireplace and thick oak pillars add even more atmosphere to its cosiness, and many paintings of All Stretton and Church Stretton in days gone by decorate the walls. A panelled oak bar serves Hobsons Best, Carling and Stella Artois lager, Guinness and a guest beer, with Stowford Press for the cider drinker. A varied menu of starters and meat, fish and vegetarian dishes is supplemented by various extras on the large specials board. The food is of outstanding quality and generous portions will ensure you don't leave hungry. The usual opening hours are kept, with food available from 12 noon to 2 pm and 7 pm to 9 pm. Telephone: 01694 722228.

The Walk

① Turn right from the pub's main door onto the road and right again into the lane signed 'Village Hall'. Walk past the village hall and a few yards further on note one of the original Tudor style cottages on the corner with the date 1603 inscribed on it.

② Just past the cottage turn left at a public footpath sign, crossing the stream and a

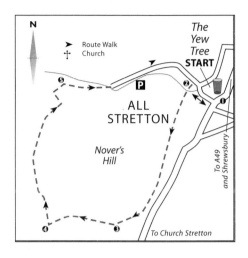

stile. Now walk ahead alongside a high wall on a well-used path across the field. At the end of the field cross a tarmac drive and continue ahead; the path is now hedged in on both sides but not overgrown. Pass through a former gateway by the last bungalow and fork right up the slope past a look-out seat. From here you get the best views. Directly opposite on the other side of the vale is Caer Caradoc, while the hill with the TV transmitter on top is Helmeth Hill and, in between, the hill covered with trees is Hazler Hill, now owned by the Woodland Trust. Walk on, passing the edge of a pine copse, and descend to a stony track.

③ Turn right. Cross the cattle grid ahead and walk on up the right track towards some houses, with a fence on your left. When the fence turns left, do likewise and walk up a short slope to a field gate with a sign 'please close gate' on it.

④ Go through the gate and after five paces forward turn right along a narrow sheep track. This soon widens a little and

View from Cwmdale

takes you above Cwmdale and its little knot of houses and smallholdings until it descends into Batch Valley by the last field. Turn right for the valley track and turn right again when you reach the stream.

⑥ You now walk straight down the valley. Cross the stream by a footbridge near Reservoir Cottage. Here there was, until the 1950s, a small reservoir which supplied All Stretton with its water. Cross the cattle grid by the National Trust sign and walk down the lane back to the pub.

PLACES OF INTEREST NEARBY

Acton Scott historic working farm, off the A49 south of Church Stretton (GR 453899) – run in the 19th century fashion with heavy horses used for ploughing, vintage machinery, rare breeds and much more of interest. There are different attractions each weekend, such as cider making, butter making and craft demonstrations. Shop and café. Open March to November. Telephone: 01694 781306/7.

Cardington
The Royal Oak

MAP: OS EXPLORER 217 (GR 507952) | **WALK 20** | **DISTANCE:** 3 MILES

DIRECTIONS TO START: CARDINGTON IS 4 MILES EAST OF CHURCH STRETTON.
FROM SHREWSBURY TAKE THE A49 SOUTH AND TURN LEFT AT LEEBOTWOOD.
PARKING: PATRONS MAY LEAVE THEIR CARS IN THE PUB CAR PARK WHILE THEY WALK;
PLEASE INFORM THE LANDLORD.

Cardington has often been described as the prettiest village in Shropshire and it is indeed very attractive. A cluster of old stone and half-timbered cottages is grouped around the part Gothic church of St James which is approximately 800 years old, with its tower visible for miles around. In spring lines of daffodils guard the approaches. The village lies in a vale between the Stretton Hills to the west and Wenlock Edge to the east.

There are no main roads nearby so it retains an air of calm and tranquillity. The views along the walk are superb; be sure to look back before you get to point 2. From Hill End look across Ape Dale to Wenlock Edge, a patchwork of fields unspoilt by developments, and beyond to Brown Clee Hill and Abdon Burf. Ahead you can see Willstone Hill, with Caer Caradoc beyond it. All the stiles and gates on this circuit bear waymarks.

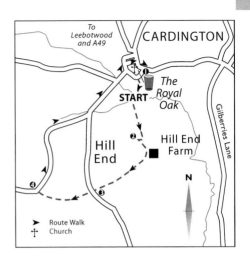

The Royal Oak

The inn, a grade II listed building, has a 'chocolate box' setting. It is tucked away on the east side of the village and very convenient for the church which is next door as the crow flies, the backdrop surmounted by beautiful trees. South-facing, the tables out front are always popular on dreamy summer days. Inside, the pub is cosy and comfortable with a high and low dining area and settles of elm. Oak beam ceilings are hung with horse brasses and the open fireplace dominates the lower bar area. The menu in this welcoming inn is vast, with something to suit every taste. There are freshly made pâtés and soups among the starters, and the main courses include Shropshire fidget pie and a lamb shank dish to which I am very partial, also a vegetarian choice. Snacks such as jacket potatoes are served too. Beers on offer include Bass, locally brewed Heaven's Sent, Hobsons and Somerset brewed Golden Arrow, with Strongbow for the cider lovers. The pub is open from 12 noon to 3 pm and 7 pm (6 pm on Friday) to 11 pm, except for Monday lunchtime (closed). Food is available during opening times until 9 pm, but not on Sunday night. Telephone/Fax: 01694 771266.

The Walk

① From the pub turn right but only as far as the first group of cottages on the left; here bear left into a narrow passage marked with a public footpath sign. In the first field fork right for the stile, cross and continue over some rough ground to a second stile, followed by a plank bridge made of old railway sleepers. Go over the bridge and turn left up the field.

② At the top of the field go through the gate and turn right for a short distance to a second gate, opening onto a farm track. At the track turn sharp left, almost doubling back on yourself. On the edge of the farmyard bear to the right up a short slope to a field gate marked with two waymarks. Go through and fork right. This path skirts round the bottom of Hill End, edged with bracken. When opposite the green barn away to your left, fork right again, through the bracken, and bear right round the end of Hill End to find a stile in the middle of a group of four trees. Go over the stile and straight across the field towards the next field gate, at the side of which is a stile which gives onto the lane to Cardington.

③ Cross the lane, unless you want to shorten the walk by going straight back to Cardington, and go over the stile opposite. Walk along by the hedge on your left to the next gate. This has three waymarks, two blue and an 'Ippikins Way' sign, the tip of

The village of Cardington clusters around St James' church

which points in the direction for you to go. From here the next gate is clearly visible. Drop down this field diagonally to that gate – there are two gates, one beyond the other – go through and continue ahead to the lane at Sharpstones.

④ Turn right down the lane. At the next road junction, turn left, signposted 'Cardington ½'. Instead of turning right to return to the pub, continue past the church and turn right after the churchyard just to see a little more of this very attractive village. When you reach the next road junction, turn right for the Royal Oak.

> **PLACES OF INTEREST NEARBY**
> **Wilderhope Manor** (National Trust), ½ mile south of the B4371 at Longville (GR 545929). Built in 1586, it is one of the finest houses in the area. Several people have seen its ghost, believed to be Francis Smallman, the original owner. The house is open from April to September on Wednesday and Saturday and from October to March on Saturday only, 2 pm to 4.30 pm, but the grounds are always open. Telephone: 0194 771363/723068.

Hilltop
The Wenlock Edge Inn

MAP: OS EXPLORER 217 (GR 570963) | WALK 21 | **DISTANCE:** 2¼ MILES

DIRECTIONS TO START: HILLTOP IS ON THE B4371 MUCH WENLOCK TO CHURCH STRETTON ROAD, 4 MILES SOUTH-EAST OF MUCH WENLOCK. **PARKING:** CUSTOMERS MAY USE THE CAR PARK AT THE INN WHILE WALKING – PLEASE ASK FIRST.

This stroll begins beside gentle rolling fields and returns along the wooded tracks and paths of the western side of Wenlock Edge. Some road walking is involved but it is easy and very quiet. Part of the route uses the old railway track which formerly ran from Craven Arms to Wellington. The whole area has a peaceful, unhurried feel to it – something to be treasured. Although the western side of Wenlock Edge is heavily wooded the return leg is on the edge of the trees and so has almost uninterrupted views. In contrast to the open, gentle fields of the eastern side, the limestone escarpment to the west is very steep and sometimes precipitous in places but there are many easily walked paths and tracks laid out and waymarked by the National Trust and the County Council.

The Wenlock Edge Inn

This is a pub not to be missed. Originally a row of 17th century cottages for quarrymen, it is now an award-winning inn with a four star English Tourist Board rosette – and its complement of ghosts. Jack Drummond is one of them, a former quarryman, who helps look after the place by moving things about and who is reputed to have told a psychic called in to investigate, 'Well, they keep putting things on my furniture!' The two comfortable lounges are cosy and welcoming, with heavy oak beams and pews and open fireplaces, one with a wood-buring stove, and there are outdoor tables on the patio and in the garden. Much of the food on offer is home made and it includes soups, baked ham, venison pie, pan fried breast of duck – to name but a few dishes – and plenty of sweets. Hobsons Best and Town Crier and Boddingtons Bitter are among the real ales, alongside Heineken lager and Stowford Press cider. Overnight accommodation is also available. The inn is open during the week from 11.30 am to 2.30 pm (not Monday) and 6.30 pm to 11 pm, although in the winter months it is closed all day on Monday and also at lunchtime on Tuesday. On Sunday the opening hours are 12 noon to 2.30 pm and 6.30 pm to 10.30 pm throughout the year. Meals are served from 12 noon to 2 pm and 7 pm to 9 pm. Telephone: 01746 785678.

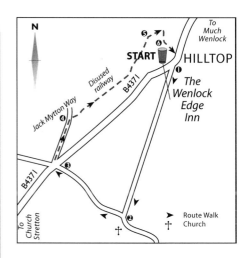

The Walk

① From the pub entrance turn left along the B4371 for a few yards only and fork left down a very quiet back lane with the blue warning sign 'unsuitable for HGVs'.

② At Easthope turn right, signposted 'Longville', but not before paying a visit to the church which, although probably locked, is set in a perfect spot, surrounded by open fields with the park of Lutwyche Hall beyond. Notice how the west side of the churchyard ends in a ha-ha, a most unusual feature.

③ Cross the main B4371 with great care, for cars come along here at great speed, and fork right along a 'no through road', signposted 'Easthope Wood'. At the foot of the hill bear left through the car park just before the railway bridge and turn right along the old trackbed.

④ This was the line from Wellington through Much Wenlock to Craven Arms. It was hardly a busy line, just three through trains a day although there was quite an intensive service as far as Much Wenlock. This stretch of the walk has splendid views, unimpeded by the trees.

The church at Easthope

⑤ At the first junction of tracks, ¹/₂ mile from the bridge, fork right uphill; there is a waymark post at the corner with a green arrow at the top and the words 'Ippikins Rock' stencilled on one side. Walk up the track to the next waymark post and here, again, turn right. Wooden steps have been made to take you up to a stile and onto the top of the Edge. Turn left. Notice there is a viewpoint if you turn right, but be warned: there is a precipitous drop beyond it so hold on to children and keep back from the edge.

⑥ Go through the wicket gate and ahead you can see the inn. Bearing slightly to the right, go through two field gates, making sure to close them after you, to reach the car park again.

PLACES OF INTEREST NEARBY
Wenlock Priory, Much Wenlock – a Cluniac monastery in the care of English Heritage, set in attractive gardens, formerly the cloisters, with striking topiary, a rare lavatorium and a Norman chapter house. Audio tour available. Open daily all year. Telephone: 01952 727466.

Ackleton
The Red Cow

DIRECTIONS TO START: ACKLETON IS 5 MILES NORTH-EAST OF BRIDGNORTH. TAKE THE WOLVERHAMPTON ROAD (A454) EAST FOR 3 MILES. JUST AFTER A FILLING STATION ON THE RIGHT, TURN LEFT, THEN QUICKLY RIGHT, SIGNPOSTED 'ALBRIGHTON'. AT THE JUNCTION WITH THE B4176 TURN LEFT, SIGNPOSTED 'TELFORD', AND AT THE FOLLY INN TURN RIGHT FOR ACKLETON. **PARKING:** THERE ARE LARGE CAR PARKS AT THE FRONT AND REAR WHICH PATRONS ARE WELCOME TO USE WHILE WALKING.

Literary buffs and lovers of a short stroll will be in their element on this walk for it is right in the heart of P.G. Wodehouse country. As a boy Wodehouse lived in Stableford and carried his love of the area right through his long writing career. He is said to have described Badger Dingle, through which this route passes, as 'the most beautiful spot in a county noted for its fine scenery'. Across this gentle countryside with its easy walking strode Lord Emsworth and his brother Galahad and now you can follow in their footsteps. Worfield, Bridgnorth, Shifnal and Weston Park (the setting for Blandings Castle) are all thinly disguised in the Blandings books. So come along and sample this really quiet rural area of north-east Shropshire, right off the tourist track, where you will find peace and tranquillity.

The Red Cow

The late 18th century Red Cow has always been a public house and was probably a coaching inn in its early days. Inside, the rooms are extremely comfortable and well furnished, with wall to wall carpeting, unvarnished oak beams covered with horse brasses and plates and panelled walls to half height. The central bar serves all three rooms, one of which is a dining area. The main bar has an open fireplace. There are a few tables outside at the front where drinks may be enjoyed but food is only served inside. The superb menu is very varied, with a good selection of meat and fish, ploughman's and lasagne, vegetarian meals and many cold dishes. Daily specials are to be found on the blackboards, together with starters and sweets. The Sunday roasts are strongly recommended. The portions here are enormous so a good appetite is essential! Banks's beer is on tap, together with Marston's Pedigree and a guest beer, plus Stella Artois, Foster's and Strongbow cider. Bookings are advisable for Sunday lunch and evening meals. The opening hours are 12 noon to 3 pm and 6 pm to 9.30 pm (closed Sunday evening and Monday lunchtime). Food is served daily from 12 noon to 1.45 pm (not Monday) and 6 pm to 9 pm (not Sunday). Telephone: 01746 783665.

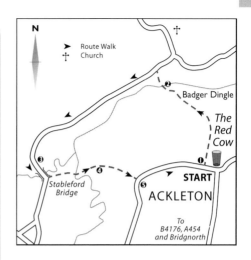

The Walk

① From the pub turn right along the lane for a few yards and then go right again by a telephone post onto a level unmade track between hedges on both sides. In a little while the track narrows but carries on in the same direction until it enters a field. Cross the field diagonally half-left in the direction indicated by the waymark post to enter Badger Dingle on a wide path which is probably a continuation of the original track.

② Cross the stream by 'Middle Pool' with a waterfall on your left and ignoring the 'tunnel' bear left over it and then turn right to follow the path up a gentle slope, leaving the stream behind you and with the gully on your right – don't follow the path down the dingle as it is not a right of way. At the lane turn left. Note the unusal thatched lychgate at the entry to the cemetery on the right.

③ Cross Stableford Bridge and turn left over the stile by a gate; there is a footpath signpost here. Stableford, where P.G. Wodehouse grew up, is a pretty village with several half-timbered buildings so take the opportunity to continue along the lane to see it if you wish. To continue the walk, from the stile by Stableford Bridge go over the field on a visible path through the grass.

The pretty village of Stableford

The stream is on your left and you eventually cross it by a very solid concrete footbridge.

④ In the second field the path is again visible in the grass and goes uphill; aim for the point where woods on the right meet a clump of gorse bushes at the top of the field. There is a stile between the woods and the gorse. Go over the stile and by another well-defined track cross the third and last field, heading towards the tip of a telephone post which is just visible from the stile. You will soon be able to see a field gate ahead and at its side is a waymarked stile.

⑤ In the lane turn left and now it's an easy walk back to the start.

PLACES OF INTEREST NEARBY

Royal Air Force Museum, Cosford (GR 790050) – from Ackleton follow the Albrighton signs. The museum houses one of the largest collections of civil and military aircraft in the country. Over 80 historic machines can be seen in three heated hangars and an outside display. Special events are held throughout the year. Telephone: 01902 376200 or information line 0870 606 2027, website www.rafmuseum.com

Bishop's Castle
The Castle Hotel

MAP: OS EXPLORER 216 (GR 325890) · **WALK 23** · **DISTANCE:** 3 MILES

DIRECTIONS TO START: BISHOP'S CASTLE IS 22 MILES SOUTH-WEST OF SHREWSBURY ON THE A488 ROAD AND 8 MILES NORTH-WEST OF CRAVEN ARMS. FROM SHREWSBURY ON THE A488, TURN RIGHT SIGNED 'B4384 BISHOP'S CASTLE', THEN TAKE SECOND RIGHT PAST THE THREE TUNS. THE CASTLE HOTEL IS STRAIGHT AHEAD. **PARKING:** IN THE HOTEL CAR PARK, WITH PERMISSION.

Far away from the hustle and bustle of modern life, the little town of Bishop's Castle is tucked away between the A49 trunk road and the Welsh border. The Bishop of Hereford certainly had the right idea when he built his castle on the highest point of the town in 1100. It lasted until the early part of the 17th century and the Castle Hotel, which now occupies the site, was built in the early 18th century. Leaving the town, this delightful stroll takes you along a country lane, a 'no through road' so traffic is rare, returning beside a gentle babbling brook, through a small copse and over a few fields with great views. This is a walk where you can breath in fresh air and just relax.

The Castle Hotel

This substantial, imposing Georgian seven-bay stone house dates from 1719. Originally a coaching inn the building is festooned with hanging baskets and tubs of flowers in summer. There are picnic tables at the front and more on the two terraced gardens at the back, with a fishpond and lovely views over the town. Pergolas, climbing plants and stonewalls complete the pleasant atmosphere outdoors. Inside it is very relaxing and quiet. The first bar you enter from the front door is a small, cosy 'snug' with an open fireplace and paintings of country scenes on the walls. Beyond this is the spacious lounge area with a wood-burning stove. Both bars have beamed ceilings and panelled walls with old local prints. The variety on the menu will satisfy anyone – from sandwiches, pâté and soups to a full blown bar meal of cod and chips, steak and kidney pie and game pie. The brews include Bass, Black Sheep, Hobsons and the locally brewed Six Bells Big Nev's (you pass the Six Bells on the walk), not to mention 36 different whiskies. Overnight accommodation is also available. Open daily from 12 noon to 2.30 pm. Evening opening hours are 6.30 pm (6 pm on Sunday) to 11 pm on Monday to Saturday and 7 pm to 10.30 pm on Sunday. Food is served daily from 12 noon to 1.30 pm and 6.30 pm (7 pm Sunday) to 8.45 pm. Telephone: 01588 638403.

The Walk

① From the hotel turn right through the town and right again at the church. On the corner is the Six Bells, which has its own

brewery. Ignore the first turning left by the church and continue ahead towards the telephone box.

② Turn left into Grange Road. At the end pass the garages and, bearing slightly left, drop down a short slope onto a metalled footpath alongside a stream. On emerging onto a lane, turn left. Pass The Ridge, a side road on your left, and then walk on for 1¹/₂ miles, passing as you do so two farms. After the second, the lane begins a gradual descent. At a gentle left-hand bend look for a gate on the left where there is a footpath sign and a Shropshire Way buzzard sign on the gatepost.

③ Walk across a long field, keeping to the left of the wooded patch in the middle. The next stile is close by the stream. Fork half-left across the next field towards woodland. A waymarked stile marks the way into the woods. The easy to follow track ascends through the trees to a field at the top.

④ On emerging from the woods you are in a large field with a field gate ahead. The

Bishop's Castle

right of way is around the depression on your left. The next stile is in the hedgerow at the top of a short bank. Cross the stile and turn sharp right to a second stile, into a larger field. Go straight ahead, heading for the corner post of the fence, which disappears over the brow of the hill. On reaching the fence, go ahead and by crossing three stiles in succession arrive at a large white cottage.

⑤ Turn left at the cottage and follow the rough track. At the end turn right and then left; at the Six Bells, turn right and then left to return to the start.

PLACES OF INTEREST NEARBY

Bishop's Castle Railway and Transport Museum is passed on the walk – open Easter to October, Saturday and Sunday, 2 pm to 5 pm and at other times by arrangement. You will find a collection of memorabillia and photographs of the railway line that closed in 1935 – a short-lived line but with many stories to tell. Telephone: 01588 660293 or 640300 (daytime).

Wistanstow
The Plough

MAP: OS EXPLORER 217 (GR 432854)　　**WALK 24**　　**DISTANCE:** 3¼ MILES

DIRECTIONS TO START: WISTANTOW IS 2 MILES NORTH OF CRAVEN ARMS. FROM SHREWSBURY TAKE THE A49 SOUTH AND TURN RIGHT A MILE AFTER THE TRAVELLERS REST PUB. **PARKING:** PATRONS MAY LEAVE THEIR CARS IN THE PUB CAR PARK WHILE THEY WALK; PLEASE INFORM THE LANDLORD.

Wistanstow, which gets its name from the martyred Mercian prince St Wystan, is built on the line of the old Roman road, Watling Street, that ran from Viroconium (Wroxeter) near Shrewsbury to Hereford. The site of the village was later taken over by the Anglo-Saxons. It is situated on high ground in the pleasant valley of the River Onny below Wenlock Edge. Most of the cottages are built of stone although the village hall is a prime example of a half-timbered building. On its outward leg the walk follows the River Onny and the former Craven Arms to Bishop's Castle railway, returning through gentle country with nice views. An easy stroll with no difficult gradients.

The Plough

The inn has been here since 1774. Take note in the entrance lobby of the display of beer bottles, not any old beers, but those specially brewed to celebrate the ill-fated wedding of Prince Charles and Diana. The main lounge is very spacious with plenty of individual tables, some in window alcoves, while parties can be accommodated in 'The Snug'. There is a non-smoking dining area. It is not every pub that can claim to have its own brewery but, with the Wood's brewery alongside, the Plough is one that does. Wood's brews are well known in Shropshire and are widely marketed; among their offerings at the Plough, are Shropshire Lad and Parish Bitter. Other beers available here are Ansells Mild and Timothy Taylor Landlord, and for the cider drinker Stowford Press and Addlestones. The food leans on English cooking with a seasonal menu. Rabbit pie is sometimes on offer, while the snacks include the justifiably famous baguettes, a great favourite with those wanting a light meal. A traditional Sunday lunch is also served. The wine list includes the locally produced Wroxeter wine from the vineyard near Shrewsbury. The opening hours during the week are 11.30 am to 2.30 pm and 6.30 pm to 11 pm (closed on Monday evenings). On Sunday the Plough is open from 12 noon to 2 pm and 7 pm to 10.30 pm. Food is served every day, except Sunday and Monday evenings, 12 noon to 2 pm and 7.30 pm to 9 pm. Telephone: 01588 673251.

The Walk

① Cross the road from the car park and walk down the lane almost opposite. Cross the main A489 to the wide grassy track opposite, marked with an 'unsuitable for motors' sign.

② Cross the footbridge and turn right over the stile, signposted 'Onny Trail'. Follow the path around the edge of the field. Cross the next stile, which is at the foot of a group of trees, and make your way to the site of a former railway bridge and to the stile beyond. From here you walk about a ½ mile along the old trackbed.

③ You shortly come to an open field, just beyond which is a gate and a stile at an oblique angle. Don't cross the stile but fork left, following the fence up the embankment. Walk up the field, with the stream just below you to your right, for only 20 yards or so before dropping down on a sheep track to cross the stream and heading up the next field to a gate to the right of a small copse. Go through it and through the

The River Onny flows through gentle countryside

next gate. Don't follow the fence; strike out up the middle of the field.

④ Pass through a line of scrub trees and go over the field towards the cottage. Cross the stile and turn left. Here there are fine views: to your left is Wenlock Edge and beyond it, to its left, surmounted by radio beacons, is Brown Clee and to its right, surmounted by a radar dome, is Titterstone Clee Hill, while behind you to the north is the Long Mynd. At the top of this track turn left and continue to Cheney Longville.

⑤ At the far end of the village, by the last cottage on the left, go ahead onto a wide grassy track. A footbridge crosses the stream and then you come to a wicket gate.

Go through and continue ahead, following waymarked stiles. At the next field gate turn left, over the stile and then continue dead ahead. On crossing the railway embankment you saw on the way out, go to a nearby stile. Turn left along the track to the footbridge you crossed earlier. Now retrace your outward steps back to the village.

PLACES OF INTEREST NEARBY

The Secret Hills Centre, Craven Arms (A49 road) is the main information centre publicising the beauties of the South Shropshire hills; it is well worth a visit. The facilities include a simulated balloon ride over the Shropshire hills as well as a well-stocked bookshop, a café, a gift shop and riverside walks. Telephone: 01588 676040.

Aston on Clun
The Kangaroo

MAP: OS EXPLORER 217 (GR 396816) | **WALK 25** | **DISTANCE:** 3¼ MILES

DIRECTIONS TO START: ASTON ON CLUN IS 24 MILES SOUTH OF SHREWSBURY AND 3 MILES WEST OF CRAVEN ARMS ON THE B4368 ROAD TO CLUN. **PARKING:** IN THE PUB CAR PARK, WITH PERMISSION.

A very easy, tranquil walk meandering along the valley to Hopesay in this quiet corner of Shropshire, through rolling countryside alive with birds. Apart from one short climb it's mostly level, and it is waymarked throughout with one exception. On a warm summer's day there can be no better place to visit. The wide, fertile Clun Valley is an area of outstanding natural beauty made famous by A.E. Housman. Aston on Clun is a very small hamlet with just the pub and a few houses. In the middle stands an English poplar – the arbour tree. On Arbour Day, 29th May, this tree is dressed with national flags of various countries, a tradition that dates back to the marriage of one Mary Carter in 1786. There are two round houses in Aston while, next to the pub, the garage was previously a blacksmith's shop.

The Kangaroo

This late 18th century coaching inn has been continuously licensed since 1831. The origin of its peculiar name is unknown, and it is the only pub with this name in England. In the 19th century there were dark doings here; poachers sold their ill-gotten gains behind locked doors and, on one occasion, Black Country horse dealers caused a riot. Now it is a cosy village pub with a warm, friendly atmosphere. Its comfortable lounges have traditional heavy oak beams and stone fireplaces. The dining room is a non-smoking area and at the back is a garden with tables. Barbecues are held on summer Saturdays. Among the beers are the locally brewed Roo Brew from Bishop's Castle and Bombardier from Bedford as well as a weekly guest beer and various lagers, Strongbow and a guest cider. The very high quality menu is sufficient for most tastes, with soup, light meals such as ploughman's, cooked dishes such as steaks, pasta, gammon and cod, and salads, plus extras on the blackboard and vegetarian food. Children's portions can be requested. The Kangaroo is closed on Monday and Tuesday lunchtimes but otherwise keeps the usual hours, with all day opening on Friday to Sunday. Food is available from Wednesday to Sunday: 12 noon to 2 pm and 7 pm to 9 pm on Wednesday and Thursday; 12 noon to 3 pm and 7 pm to 9 pm on Friday and Saturday; 12 noon to 3 pm on Sunday. Telephone: 01588 660263.

The Walk

① From the pub turn left. In the middle of the village is the arbour tree. Cross the road by the phone box and go straight ahead up the lane, signposted to Hopesay and Edgton. Turn left after the bungalow, Wyndale, onto a wide grassy track; there is no 'public bridleway' sign – this is the one exception I mentioned. You now walk along a level grassy track hedged in on both sides for ¹/₂ mile.

② Go through the wicket gate at the end of the track and, at the junction of tracks, turn right. The bridleway now continues along a sunken track that can be wet, even sometimes in summer, as a stream runs down part of it. Continue ahead through the next field until you come to a wicket gate.

③ Go through the gate and keep on the track, which soon widens out and takes you down to the lane on the edge of Hopesay.

④ Turn right along the lane for 50 yards, pass the last house on the left, Fairmead,

A lovely view to be enjoyed on the route

and turn left at an old iron kissing gate by the footpath signpost. Go straight ahead, crossing the footbridge and the stile beyond it, and make your way up the field to a second iron kissing gate at the top by the trees. Go through and turn right downhill past the cottage.

⑤ Go over the stile, turn right, then almost immediately turn left through a third iron gate and pass uphill through a small copse. Aston on Clun is now straight ahead. After crossing a wide field there is a boggy patch in the next copse but you can skirt round it by keeping lower down.

⑥ Keep ahead in the next field, passing two waymark posts, to join a grassy track

shortly passing a cottage and then, at the lane, continue ahead to return to the village and to the pub.

PLACES OF INTEREST NEARBY

Stokesay Castle, 1 mile south of Craven Arms. A most perfectly preserved fortified 13th century manor house in the care of English Heritage. Open daily from April to October; Wednesday to Sunday from November to March. Telephone: 01588 672544. **Bury Ditches Hill Fort and Country Park** (GR 327837) covers about 7 acres and has superb views and impressive fortications. There are plenty of colour coded walks, also a car park and picnic area. From Aston on Clun go west along the B4368 to Clunton and turn right; it is signed from there. Always open.

The Down
The Down Inn

MAP: OS EXPLORER 218 (GR 685905)   **WALK 26**   DISTANCE: 2 OR 3 MILES

DIRECTIONS TO START: FROM BRIDGNORTH TAKE THE B4364 LUDLOW ROAD.
THE DOWNS INN IS ON THIS ROAD 3 MILES SOUTH-WEST OF BRIDGNORTH.
PARKING: PATRONS ARE WELCOME TO USE THE LARGE CAR PARK AT THE PUB WHILE
WALKING; PLEASE ASK FIRST.

Rolling fields and endless views will delight you on this stroll. The pub is situated on high ground and the route takes advantage of this, particularly on the outward stretch. This is a very gentle walk, with no hard climbs anywhere and roughly level throughout. As you get to the higher ground the view is even better and to the south you can seen Brown Clee Hill. The masts are on a sub section of the hill called Abdon Burf where, until the middle of the last century, there were extensive quarrying activities which included a complete railway system linked by a rope incline to the valley below; the incline can still be seen and walked today. You pass through two hamlets that bear the name Eudon, Eudon Burnell and Eudon George, both of which are nothing more than a few houses and a farm or two.

The Down Inn

The word which comes to mind on stepping through the door of this pub is 'opulence'. Carpeted from wall to wall, muddy boots outside please, it exudes comfort and quality – look at those lush blue chairs and window seats which look out onto open countryside, no wonder they need such a big car park. Everything about the interior gives a feeling of spaciousness and privacy; the tables aren't crowded together and you can move about, even when it's busy, with ease. The exact age of this remote inn isn't known, it's that old! Greatly extended in the 1960s the extensions perfectly match the original part, with thick oak beams and undressed stonewalls, all beautifully done. The menu is quite something too: all the usual starters and main meals of fish and meat, including home-made steak pie and lamb shank, also vegetarian dishes and salads. At lunchtime there are also snacks available such as sandwiches, jacket potatoes, steak toasties, turkey and ham pie and many more. Two guest beers change weekly, the resident beers being Banks's, alongside Guinness, Fosters, and Stella Artois lager and Strongbow cider, also red and white wine on tap. Opening times are Tuesday to Saturday 12 noon to 2.30 pm and 6 pm to 11 pm; Sunday 12 noon to 2.30 pm and 7 pm to 10.30 pm (closed all day Monday). Food is served on Tuesday to Saturday from 12 noon to 2 pm and 6.30 pm to 9 pm (10 pm on Saturday) and on Sunday from 12 noon to 2.30 pm and 7 pm to 9 pm. Telephone: 01746 789539.

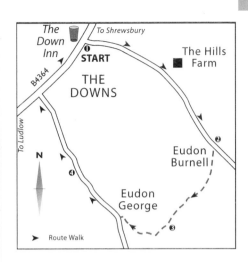

The Walk

① From the pub turn left along the main road for a few yards and turn first right, signposted 'Eudon'. It is along this lane that you get the best views, for starters look to the left. Pass the farm and continue along the lane. Gaps in the hedge on the right give further great views south and it is from the last of these when opposite The Hills Farm that you can see south to Brown Clee.

② There is nothing to tell you when you reach the hamlet of Eudon Burnell but there is a lone house on the left and a 'cattle' road sign just beyond it. Just after the road sign, turn right through an open gateway and follow a waymarked track alongside the hedge, which is on your left now. Go straight ahead, passing to the left of a pond, and continue ahead when the field boundary bends left by a patch of nettles. You will be able to see a white cottage beyond the trees straight ahead; keep on a direct course for the cottage.

The track by South Eudon Farm

③ The field drops down to a line of trees which border a stream. Go just a few steps left to find a wide gap and a footpath between the stream and the trees which takes you through a few nettles to a footbridge. Cross and walk up a short slope by way of a gully to pass that white cottage, Ratford. On reaching the gate at the end of the drive continue ahead away from the cottage. Go left on reaching the barn at South Eudon Farm and at the lane turn right.

④ Continue along the lane to the main road and there turn right. It is not a very busy road but traffic is fast so keep to the right and use the verge when traffic approaches.

PLACES OF INTEREST NEARBY

Rays Farm Country Matters, Billingsley (5 miles south-east of The Down (GR 714833) – from the pub drive through Eudon Burnell and turn right on the B4363. A collection of unusual farm animals and birds, with two woodland walks, also a teashop. Telephone: 01299 841255, website www.stargate-uk.co.uk/adverts/rays.html.

Chelmarsh
The Bull's Head

MAP: OS EXPLORER 218 (GR 722876) | **WALK 27** | **DISTANCE:** 3½ MILES

DIRECTIONS TO START: CHELMARSH IS 4 MILES SOUTH OF BRIDGNORTH. TAKE THE B4363, THEN THE B4555, SIGNPOSTED 'CHELMARSH'. **PARKING:** PATRONS ARE WELCOME TO USE THE PUB CAR PARK WHILE WALKING; PLEASE ASK FIRST.

I love this walk. It is situated on the western side of the Severn Vale and principally on high ground with the result that almost throughout there are breathtaking views over the vale to the east and on the return stretch to the west as well. In addition you skirt the edge of Chelmarsh Reservoir, a nature reserve, and if you are a keen bird watcher you can extend the walk to include a visit to the two public hides. Chelmarsh itself is perched above the vale but now shows no sign of its busy past when damson orchards clothed its slopes and the menfolk of the village went off to the nearby coalmines. I have heard that, even today, you can sometimes meet the miners coming back from their toils!

The Bull's Head

Having opened in the 17th century, the Bull's Head, which commands a prime position midway along the straggling village street, probably did sterling work as a local for the thirsty miners after their hours underground but now it exudes an air of serenity and gracious living. There are three large rooms: the dining area, which is non-smoking, includes the conservatory looking out over the Severn Vale, and the two main bars are spacious and comfortable with stonewalls, wood-burning stoves and beamed ceilings hung with brasses. Outside are small, well-kept lawns with many tables for outdoor meals on a summer day, all enjoying the splendid view over the river valley. Bar snacks include sandwiches with a choice of fillings, soup and jacket potatoes and the lunch menu has shepherd's pie, beef stew, roast chicken, vegetarian dishes and much more, supplemented by a specials board. There is an extensive restaurant menu, also a children's menu. Various beers are on offer, including Boddingtons, alongside Stella Artois and Heineken lager, Murphy's and Strongbow cider on draught. The inn offers overnight accommodation and several self-catering houses of some elegance surround the car park. Opening times are daily from 12 noon to 2.30 pm and 7 pm to 11 pm. Food is available from 12 noon to 2.30 pm and 6.30 pm to 9.30 pm every day, including Sunday. Telephone: 01746 861469.

The Walk

① Turn left from the pub and walk north. Just after the T junction sign cross the road

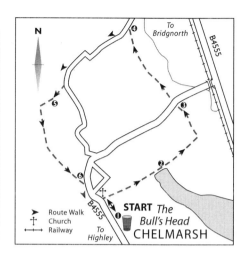

and walk down a tarred bridleway. Pass to the right of Hall Farm, continuing downhill on a stony track.

② You come to Chelmarsh Reservoir. The noticeboard shows you where to go to find the hides and what birds you may expect to see. Continue walking ahead over the reservoir dam and up a short slope to Dinney Barn, now a house. Continue ahead along the metalled farm lane to the main road.

③ Cross the main road to a hardcore track directly opposite. Go past the barns and, crossing a stile, head across the parkland of Astbury Hall to the tarmac drive and pass a waymark post. At the top of the rise is a waymarked stile. Go over and strike out across the field. There are two more waymark posts in the field. Stay on the high ground and head for the house you can see in the distance.

④ At the lane turn left and continue. The lane drops down into a shallow valley where it turns sharp right then left whence

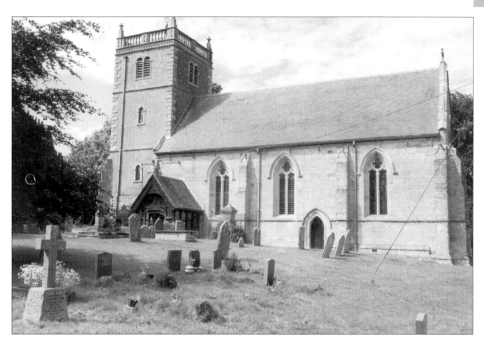

The church at Chelmarsh

it rises gently. At the next left turn go straight ahead at a public footpath signpost, using a hardcore track on the edge of a large field; the hedge is on your left and the white chimneys of Cleedsmore Farm are just visible to your right.

⑤ Where this track bends to the right turn left. Go through the gate but then immediately turn right on another green lane. At the next stile turn left and with the hedge on your left go ahead until, passing close to a triangulation pillar, you reach Manor Farm. The best views are to be enjoyed from here to both east and west.

⑥ Keep to the right of the last barn and continue ahead to a gate and stile. Cross the last field towards the road; the stile is in the far left-hand corner. Turn right to return to the start. There is no footpath for a few yards so keep to the right to face oncoming traffic.

PLACES OF INTEREST NEARBY

Daniel's Mill, Bridgnorth (GR 718918) – a working water mill with the largest waterwheel powering a corn mill still working. It is situated on the B4555 road between Eardington and Bridgnorth; follow the brown tourist signs. See wheat being turned into flour in the traditional way. There are conducted tours, also a gift shop and café. Open Easter to September. Telephone: 01746 762753.

Bucknell
The Baron of Beef

DIRECTIONS TO START: BUCKNELL IS 10 MILES DUE WEST OF LUDLOW. USE THE A4113 KNIGHTON ROAD AND TURN RIGHT AFTER BRAMPTON BRYAN, THEN TURN LEFT AFTER THE RAILWAY, SIGNPOSTED 'CHAPEL LAWN 3'. FROM CRAVEN ARMS ALSO FOLLOW THE 'KNIGHTON' ROAD SIGNS ON THE B4368 AND THEN THE B4367; CONTINUE AHEAD AT THE STATION. **PARKING:** PATRONS MAY USE THE INN CAR PARK WHILE WALKING, BUT PLEASE INFORM THE LANDLORD.

This is perfect walking country, with no traffic to spoil the peace of the area. Starting alongside the River Redlake, the route takes you gently over the high ground behind the pub by a green lane which is very easily graded and affords fine views to the village and beyond before returning by a short metalled lane and a couple of fields. The forested hills beyond make an attractive backdrop to this most enjoyable stroll.

Bucknell is a largish and very attractive village set in the south-west corner of Shropshire near the Herefordshire and Welsh borders. Its centrally-placed church, which stands on a circular raised site surrounded by yew trees, has a most unusual blue enamelled clock. With the coming of the railway Bucknell became a bustling and lively place supporting numerous trades including a corn mill, a coal depot and numerous shops and pubs.

The Baron of Beef

This grade II listed former stone barn stands near the banks of the River Redlake. The no-smoking 'Cider Bar' is the main dining area and noted for its comfort and unique décor. Situated in the centre is an enormous cider press and millstone which date from 1777 and form the focal point of the room. The original roof timbers of the barn are exposed and the walls are covered with old prints and artificial floral decorations including corn stooks which look very much at home in these surroundings. This is just one of the three comfortable bars, the others being the lounge bar with its open fireplace and the Stable Bar with its pool table. There is also an upstairs restaurant. Outside is a large lawn with tables and a children's play area. Greene King bitter is served, alongside Grolsch lager, Weston's medium sweet cider and Stowford Press. The extensive menu – I counted over 100 items – caters for every taste, offering excellent bar meals, a good selection of vegetarian dishes, starters and desserts, as well as baguettes and jacket potates, salads, ploughman's and children's dishes. There is also a weekend carvery. The Baron of Beef is open daily – usual hours – and food is available at lunchtime, from 12 noon to 2.30 pm (3 pm at weekends) and every evening from 6.30 pm to 9.30 pm. Telephone: 01547 530549.

The Walk

① Turn right from the pub drive and in a few yards fork right along Bridgend Lane. The River Redlake keeps company with you; ignore the footbridge on the left and

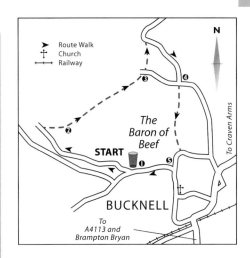

continue until the road swings round to the right with a notice on the telephone post in front which says 'Hillside Cottage'. The lane has now become a level grassy track.

② Follow the track past Hillside Cottage and straight ahead through three facing gates with extensive views to your right and steep fields on your left with patches of gorse. At the second gate you can see the pub directly below you and the church steeple rising from behind the trees in the centre of the village. This is a lovely part of the walk and dry underfoot even in wet weather.

③ At a junction of tracks, turn left and then in just a few yards turn right, still on a level, dry track, and soon pass a solitary house, Little Mynd. Now the track drops down a gentle grassy slope to a lane. Turn right and walk along the lane to a T junction with a signpost saying 'Bucknell' to the left.

④ Go straight over to the facing field gate by a bridleway sign and continue ahead.

Perfect walking country around Bucknell

The hedge is on your right and the track is between the hedge and the row of scrub trees but it may be muddy so stay in the field alongside the trees. At the end of the line of trees, at a field gate, go through the wicket gate alongside it, and continue straight on down the field with the stream nearby on your left. At the bottom of the field, near the back garden of a bungalow, drop down left to the stream on a gentle footpath and then through another wicket gate into the road. Turn right.

⑤ At the end of Dogkennel Lane turn right for the pub.

PLACES OF INTEREST NEARBY

Clun Castle (reached via Chapel Lawn and the A488 to Clun), in the care of English Heritage, is free and always open. Originally established in the years after the Norman Conquest, it was the seat of the Fitzallen family from the 12th to the 16th century and now belongs to one of their descendents, the Duke of Norfolk. Telephone: 01604 730320.

Ludlow
The Unicorn

MAP: OS EXPLORER 203 (GR 512754)   **WALK 29**   **DISTANCE:** 2½ MILES

DIRECTIONS TO START: LUDLOW IS 28 MILES SOUTH OF SHREWSBURY ON THE A49. GO INTO THE TOWN PROPER BY THE B4361. THE UNICORN IS IN LOWER CORVE STREET.
PARKING: ON THE MAIN ROAD AFTER THE A4117 TURNING TO KIDDERMINSTER OR BEHIND TESCO'S, CORVE STREET (PAY AND DISPLAY).

Ludlow has been described as one of the most perfect English towns, and it has no less than 469 listed buildings – which must surely be a record for somewhere of this size. Its origins are hidden in the past; perhaps it started out as a crossing place for the River Teme. It grew to importance after the Norman Conquest when the castle was built. This bustling market town has retained its rich architecture and character, which will be seen to advantage in Broad Street, described by Pevsner as 'one of the most memorable streets in England', and around the Market Square, both of which you visit on this walk. A brief stroll outside the town takes you over Whitcliffe with superb views. Around Ludlow on two sides runs the River Teme, which you cross twice by two delightful bridges, both in keeping with the architectural beauties of the town.

The Unicorn

Situated on the banks of the River Corve the 17th centuy Unicorn must be one of the most comfortable town pubs here – or anywhere else for that matter – as it has the atmosphere more of a relaxed country inn. Very popular with visitors and locals alike, the main bar area has oak beams, partially panelled walls and a huge open fireplace. The restaurant also has a beamed ceiling and is a no-smoking zone. At busy times there is also the Griffin Lounge which overlooks the river. For outside eating there are several tables on a small patio area directly adjacent to the riverbank. Two large blackboards advertise the vast menu on offer, including a variety of fish and meat dishes, from rabbit and home cooked ham to more intricate meals for the gourmet palate. There is also some interesting vegetarian food, while for quick bar snacks you will find jacket potatoes and sandwiches. To quench your thirst there is M&B Mild, Hancock's HB and Morland Old Speckled Hen beers, also Stowford Press and Scrumpy Jack ciders. The Unicorn is open at lunchtime from 12 noon to 2.30 pm (3.30 pm at weekends) and in the evening from 6 pm to 11 pm (7 pm to 10.30 pm on Sunday). Food is available from 12 noon to 2.15 pm and 6 pm (7 pm on Sunday) to 9.15 pm. Telephone: 01584 873555.

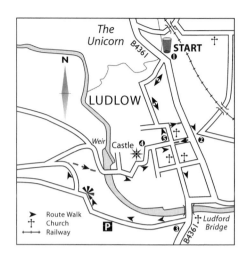

The Walk

① From the pub turn right. Cross the main road into the lane signposted 'Riverside Park'. Follow this lane round several bends until you come to a short slope with railings on one side and a short flight of steps at the top. Turn left into Upper Linney, a narrow street with a cobbled strip down the middle. Where the cobbles end, turn right into College Street. Note the plaque on the wall on the left and the section of town wall visible through the grating. Opposite the almshouses turn left through the churchyard. There are good views over the wall here. Cross the churchyard and go through the narrow archway and down the steps to emerge into Corve Street opposite the Feather's Hotel, the most photographed building in Ludlow. Turn right.

② Bear right by the HSBC bank into King Street. At the Butter Cross, the traditional heart of Ludlow, dating from 1744, turn left into Broad Street with its elegant buildings on either side. Pass through Broad Gate which dates back to the 13th century and continue across Ludford Bridge, beyond which you turn right.

③ Follow the flight of steps to Whitcliffe Common. At the first fork of paths

A chance to rest and admire the superb view over Ludlow

continue ahead; the right fork goes down to the river and can be used as a short cut to Dinham Bridge. There are superb views all along this common and many seats to enable you to rest and admire the view. Having passed the viewpoint, follow the road downhill. Near the bottom turn hard right onto a narrow footpath, waymarked 'Mortimer Trail', which descends through the woods to emerge at Dinham Bridge. Cross the bridge and go straight ahead.

④ At the entrance to Ludlow Castle turn right into the Market Square. Cross the Square heading for Church Street, the narrow street ahead on the left. It is a typical narrow street of old Ludlow, the houses between it and the adjacent parallel street are infills.

⑤ At the Church Inn turn left along College Street once more and retrace your steps to the start.

PLACES OF INTEREST NEARBY

The 900 year old **Ludlow Castle** (in the care of English Heritage) is one of the most interesting castles in England. High above the river with splendid views, it has great potential for entertaining children. One can climb the stairs to the very top of the tower. Various attractions are held here throughout the year. Telephone: 01584 873355.

Cleobury Mortimer
The King's Arms Hotel

MAP: OS EXPLORER 203 (GR 673758)   WALK 30   **DISTANCE:** 2¾ MILES

DIRECTIONS TO START: CLEOBURY MORTIMER IS 12 MILES EAST OF LUDLOW ON THE A4117 BEWDLEY/KIDDERMINSTER ROAD. **PARKING:** FREE PUBLIC CAR PARK BEHIND THE CHURCH.

This gentle stroll along the vale of the River Rea takes you to the attractive church at Neen Savage. It is an undulating route with excellent views. The most noticeable feature is the church spire of St Mary's which acts as a beacon on the return stretch of the walk. This dominates the landscape and on closer inspection it can be seen to be twisted due to the warping of the timbers. Cleobury is a village in the old style, with its local baker, butcher and more pubs than I care to count. Situated high above the river, it was not always such a quiet place as it has an industrial heritage. Elizabeth I's favourite, Robert Dudley, was responsible for an iron foundry which smelted the locally mined iron ore, and such activities as coal mining and paper making continued until Victorian times. There were many forges and mills along the river, two of which are still shown on maps.

The King's Arms Hotel

The King's Arms is an old coaching inn which fronts onto the street directly opposite the church. The highly polished oak floors and thick beams are a feature of the bar area with its large inglenook fireplace and high backed oak settles. Bar meals are usually served in here but can be taken in the non-smoking restaurant area, space permitting, if desired. Outside at the back is a small paved area with tables and a barbecue while on the lawn below there's a children's play area, just the ticket on a sunny day. The opening hours are from 11.30 am to 11 pm on Monday to Saturday and 12 noon to 10.30 pm on Sunday. Food is available at lunchtime on Monday to Friday from 12 noon to 3 pm and at weekends from 12 noon to 5 pm. In the evening it is served from 6.30 pm – booking essential on Saturdays. The bar menu includes home-made soup, pork in cider, fish pie and a vegetarian choice, as well as lighter bites such as jacket potatoes, home-made baguettes with a variety of fillings and ploughman's. There is a children's menu and on Sunday a traditional roast lunch is on offer. Among the wide selection of beers you will find the locally brewed Hobsons Town Crier and Best Bitter, Guinness, Tetley, and Strongbow and Scrumpy Jack cider. Overnight accommodation is available. Telephone: 01299 271968.

The Walk

① From the pub turn right and walk east along Church Street. Pass the phone box and the Bell Inn and take the next road left, New Road. Soon fork right again into

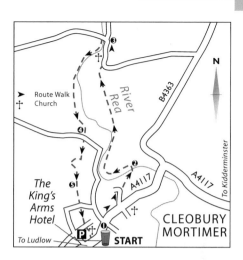

Rockley Bank and in just a few steps continue ahead at the footpath signpost on a grassy track which drops downhill to the river.

② Cross the substantial footbridge and go ahead. Turn left at the edge of the field by the cottages. The path, with the river away to your left, now follows the gentle bend in the river. Cross the stile by Walford Bridge Cottage and continue ahead; don't cross the river here. The narrow path widens beyond the cottage and becomes a green lane, taking you to Neen Savage.

③ A walk round the church is rewarded by fine views. Note the field below; you will cross it shortly. Now return to the lane and turn left. At the ford turn left over the footbridge and then left again at a stile and public footpath sign. Bear half-right across the long field you saw from the church, the gate of which is in the far right-hand corner. Go through into a short field and find the stile on the right; the path beyond climbs up a short steep slope through trees. At the green lane turn left and pass

The church at Neen Savage

Musbatch, joining the metalled farm track.

④ At the T junction go ahead over a stile and walk down the field with the hedge on your right to the stile in the corner by Cleanlyseat Farm. Now turn right and walk a short way to find a footbridge. Cross the river (a tributary of the River Rea) and walk up a short slope into a field. Go ahead at first but don't leave by the first gates; instead bear right up the field, passing a cattle trough at the back of a bungalow, and the exit is just beyond.

⑤ Now walk straight ahead, passing the school, and ahead again, passing some houses. At the next road, turn right and in a few yards you will come back to the car park.

PLACES OF INTEREST NEARBY
Mamble Craft Centre (GR 690716), 3 miles south of Cleobury Mortimer, is housed in 17th century barns and has a wonderfully tranquil setting. Tea room, craft gallery and gift shop. Open 10.30 am to 5 pm on Tuesday to Sunday and bank holidays. Telephone: 01299 832834.